This is Christianity

Book 2

The Christian Church

Michael Keene

Stanley Thornes (Publishers) Ltd

First published in 1995 by:
Stanley Thornes (Publishers) Ltd
Ellenborough House
Wellington Street
CHELTENHAM GL50 1YW
England

99 00 / 10 9 8 7 6 5

A catalogue record for this book is available from the British Library.

ISBN 0 7487 1665 3

Printed and bound in China by Dah Hua Printing Press Co. Ltd.

Acknowledgements

With thanks to the following for permission to reproduce photographs and illustrations:
Andes Press Agency/Carlos Reyes-Manzo, p.25, 35 (top), 40, 48, 64, 65, 70; ASAP/Lev Borodulin, p.66; Ateliers et Presses de Taizé, p.49 (left); Bridgeman Art Library, p.37, 59; Collections/Brian Shuel, p.53; Glasgow City Museums and Art Galleries, p.74; Geoff Howard, p.5 (top); Alexander Keene/Joanna Maclennan, p.5 (bottom), 6, 7, 8, 9, 10, 11, 12 (left), 13, 14, 15, 17, 18, 19, 20, 22, 23, 24, 26, 27, 28, 29, 31, 32, 33, 34, 35 (centre, left to right), 36, 38, 39, 42, 43, 44, 45 (right), 46 (right), 50 (bottom), 51, 52, 54, 55, 56 (left), 57, 58, 60, 62, 63, 71, 72, 73, 75, 77, 79; London City Mission/Peter Trainer, p.21; Mansell Collection, p.12 (right); Metropolitan Cathedral of Christ the King, Liverpool. Designed by Sister Anthony. Photo: John Mills, p.61; Tony Morrison, p.50 (top); Network/Jonathan Olley, p.41; Network/Paul Reas, p.67; Redferns, p.46 (left); Spacecharts, p.45 (left); Spectrum Colour Library, p.49 (right).

All other photographs supplied by the author.

Designed and typestyled by Janet McCallum
Illustrated by Gillian Hunt and Mark Dunn (pages 35 and 73)
Cover illustration by Ian Kennedy

Bible quotations are taken from the following versions:
Revised English Bible © Oxford University and Cambridge University Press, 1989.
New International Version, © 1973, 1978, 1984 by International Bible Society.
Used by permission of Hodder & Stoughton Ltd. All rights reserved.
Authorized version of the Bible (The King James Bible) the rights in which are vested in the Crown, are reproduced by permission of the Crown's Patentee, Cambridge University Press.

Contents

One Church - Many Churches
Why are there so many Churches?

Have you ever walked around your locality and noticed how many different churches there are and that they all have different names? Roman Catholic, Church of England, Methodist, Baptist, United Reformed, Salvation Army, Pentecostal – the chances are you will find them all somewhere nearby.

You might ask why all Christians cannot worship together under the same roof. We will look at that question later. But it is important to remember the fact that all Christians, whichever Church they belong to, are followers of Jesus of Nazareth.

The early Christian Church

Jesus was born as a Jew in Palestine 2000 years ago. Almost everything that we know about him comes from the pages of the New Testament. We learn that, after living a mere 33 years, Jesus was put to death by the Roman governor, Pontius Pilate. Shortly afterwards Jesus came back to life and the Christian Church was born. In the centuries that followed the Church has grown in three different stages:

Stage one

The disciples of Jesus began to preach that Jesus had been brought back to life again and that he was God's Son. A few Jews believed this and became followers of Jesus but the vast majority did not. It was from those who did believe that the Christian Church was born and it was not very long before non-Jews were being included as well.

Stage two

Within three centuries what had seemed impossible had happened: the Roman Empire had converted to Christianity. Even when that Empire suddenly crumbled in the fifth century Christianity continued to make many new converts. Then, in 1054, the Great Schism took place when churches in Eastern Europe broke away from those in the West. The Eastern Churches called themselves **Orthodox** and set up their headquarters in Constantinople. The Western Church (the **Roman Catholic Church**) had its headquarters in Rome. Once there was one Church, now there were two.

Stage three

In the sixteenth century the Reformation took place. Almost overnight the Church split up into many groups. The **Protestant Church** was formed from those people who were totally dissatisfied with the Catholic Church. Can you work out how it got its name?

In England King Henry VIII rebelled against the **Pope** in Rome, called himself the Head of the Church in England and brought the **Church of England** into existence. When this Church spread to many other countries it became known as the **Anglican Church**.

'Protestant' is an umbrella-term which covers many different Churches. Amongst them are the Methodists, the Baptists, the Quakers and the Salvation Army. You will find out more about each of these Churches later.

The Church today

Until the Reformation the Church was strongest in Europe, although there were Churches in North Africa and the Middle East and probably elsewhere as well. Then Christian missionaries began to travel across the world making new converts. They did their job so well that the Christian Church is now to be found in almost every country in the world. At the same time the Church has splintered to such an extent that there are now more than 20 000 different Christian **denominations** across the world. Some of them are very small but others, like the Roman Catholic and Anglican Churches, have millions of followers.

In this unit we are going to look at the most well-known of the Christian Churches. If, however, a smaller Church appeals to you, then carry out some research of your own into its history, beliefs and ways of worshipping.

- How was the Christian Church born?
- What took place in 1054 which had a considerable impact on the Church?
- What was the Reformation?

1 Each of these photographs shows a different Christian denomination. There is a clue in each to show which Church it is. Can you work them out?

a

b

c

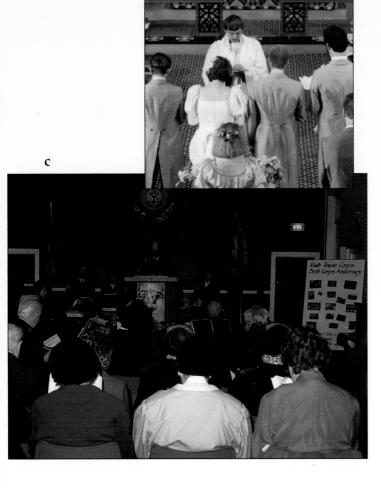

2 Here are some facts and figures for you to look at:

Total world population	5 500 000 000
Total Christian believers	1 500 000 000

Which Church do they belong to?

Roman Catholic	900 000 000
Protestant	300 000 000
Orthodox	175 000 000
Others	125 000 000

Where are they to be found?

Europe	425 000 000
South America	400 000 000
Africa	250 000 000
North America	250 000 000
Asia	150 000 000
Elsewhere	25 000 000

(Figures taken from *World Christian Handbook*, 1992)

Now answer these questions:
a Which Christian Church:
   has the largest number of followers?
   has the second largest number of followers?
b On which continent:
   are the greatest number of Christians found?
   are the second highest number of Christians found?

What is the Orthodox Church?

There are not many Orthodox Churches in the UK but worldwide the Orthodox Church today has:

- 150 000 000 members who belong to the Eastern Orthodox Church, including the Russian, Romanian and Serbian Orthodox Churches. The overall leader of this Church is the **Ecumenical Patriarch** of Constantinople, All Holiness Dmitrios. He is based in Istanbul, Turkey.

- 25 000 000 members belonging to the much smaller, but older, Oriental Orthodox Church. Five Churches belong to this branch of the family.

What is the Orthodox Church?

The word 'Orthodox' means 'true or right belief and worship'. Orthodox Christians trace their origins all the way back to the time of Jesus. The Eastern churches and Rome separated in 1054 after a row about the authority of the Pope – the Great Schism. The Eastern Churches established themselves in countries such as Russia, Armenia and Greece. After their row with Rome they would not give absolute power to any of their leaders. Even the Patriarch of Constantinople is just one leader among many.

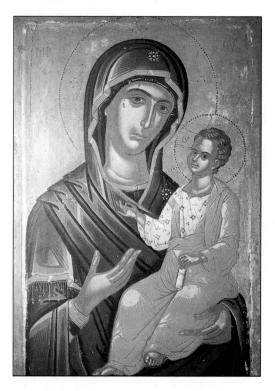

What are the religious paintings in an Orthodox church called?

What is distinctive about the Orthodox Church?

The first thing to say about the Orthodox Church is that it has changed very little over the centuries. This is a cause of great pride to its worshippers. Can you think why? It has achieved this by taking its teaching and worship from two main sources, neither of which change:

- the Holy Scriptures

- the Tradition of the Church.

Part of this tradition is the style of worship which is common to all Orthodox churches. Whilst the different branches of the Orthodox Church have their own traditions and customs they share with each other a living tradition of worship. This means that you can go into any Orthodox church and you will find yourself caught up in a service which makes full use of all your senses, through incense, chanting, singing and **icons**. Icons are religious paintings which have been produced with the greatest possible care. They become windows through which each worshipper is able to glimpse God. The worshippers treat them with

This shows an Orthodox church. How many features can you recognise from the photograph?

great respect, bowing before them and kissing them during the service. You will find many icons in an Orthodox church.

The most important Orthodox service, the **Liturgy**, is celebrated every Sunday and on festival days. Through this service the birth, death and resurrection of Jesus are re-created.

Inside an Orthodox church

As they worship each Orthodox believer is reminded of the beautiful universe in which they live by the church itself. The ceiling of the church, with large icons of Jesus, represents the heavens. Why do you think that icons are in the ceiling? The floor of the church represents the world. There are no seats in most Orthodox churches.

The most holy part of the church is the **altar** – the place where God is. A large screen (the iconostasis)

What is the name of this screen and why does it obscure the altar?

stands between the people and the altar. The screen is covered with icons. Through it the people can just glimpse the altar. The priest alone can open the Royal Doors and venture behind the screen. Why do you think this is?

- What does the word 'Orthodox' mean?
- What are the two sources of authority for the Orthodox Church?
- Why is the shape and design of an Orthodox church important?

1 One great Orthodox leader said:

'We keep the Tradition just as we received it.'

What do you think he meant when he used the word 'Tradition'?

2 Alison is 35 years old and has been attending a Russian Orthodox Church for six years. Here she describes why she was attracted to this form of worship in the first place.

'It was a great surprise to me to attend my first Orthodox service – everything was so different to my old church. The incense, the singing, the icons, the magnificent building and the feeling of peace were the ingredients that made the service so special. It is still special. Every time that I enter an Orthodox church it has the same effect on me. It makes me very conscious of God's blessing – God the Holy One.'

For your dictionary

The **altar** is the holiest part of the church. It is the place where God is.
The **Ecumenical Patriarch** is the leader of the Orthodox Church.
An **icon** is a painting or a mosaic of Jesus or one of the saints.
A **Liturgy** is a divine service which follows a set pattern.

Why do you think that the Orthodox Church and its worship had such an effect on Alison?

What is the Roman Catholic Church?

The Roman Catholic Church dates back to **Simon Peter**, the disciple whom Jesus called 'the rock'. Catholics believe that Simon Peter was not only the first leader of the Christian Church but also the first Bishop of Rome. Indeed, so great was Peter's importance in those days that he came to be regarded as the keeper of the keys of heaven. His symbol became a bunch of keys and this is reflected in the Pope's traditional emblem of a bunch of keys which underline his authority. Catholics believe he is the successor of Peter and this gives the Pope greater authority than any other Church leader.

The Roman Catholic Church

The Roman Catholic Church is the largest Christian denomination. In fact, over 50 per cent of the world's Christians are Roman Catholics. This is how the Roman Catholic Church is organised:

- the Pope has supreme authority. He lives in a small area of Italy known as the Vatican City.

- **Cardinals** are appointed to advise the Pope on Church matters.

- Bishops look after all the churches in their area (called a 'diocese'). One other large Church has bishops. Do you know which it is?

- Parish priests look after individual churches.

- Deacons help priests with their duties.

To the ordinary Catholic, however, the person who really matters is the parish priest. He conducts the all-important service of the **Mass**. He also baptises their children; conducts weddings; visits them when they are sick and buries them when they die. In each of these ways he brings God's blessing to the people. Each of these activities is called a **sacrament** and there are seven such sacraments available to Catholics:

1 **Baptism** All babies born into Catholic families are baptised as soon as possible after they are born. Can you find out why there is such a hurry?

2 *Holy Communion* When baptised children are about seven years old they take their first Communion. After this they can share fully in the great Catholic celebration of the Mass.

3 **Confirmation** This takes place when baptised children are about twelve years old. At this age they are thought to be old enough to make their own commitment to Christ and to the Church.

4 *Marriage*

5 *Confession* Personal confession of sins to God through a priest is an important Catholic activity.

6 *Ordination* This takes place when trained men are made priests by their local bishop.

7 *Holy Unction* The sick and the dying are anointed with holy oil to bring them comfort and healing of the soul.

Can you find out who the Virgin Mary is and why she plays such an important part in Roman Catholic worship?

The Second Vatican Council

The greatest changes in the Roman Catholic Church for centuries took place as a result of the Second Vatican Council. Since this Council, held between 1960 and 1965, the Mass is no longer conducted in Latin, as it had been for centuries, but in the language of the people. The Council also gave monks and nuns permission to abandon their traditional habits to wear the same clothes as the people around them, if they wanted to.

Many things, especially beliefs, did not change in the Catholic Church and this offers comfort and security to its millions of members.

- To which disciple of Jesus do Roman Catholics trace the beginning of their Church?
- Who is the leader of the Roman Catholic Church?
- What is a sacrament and how many of them are recognised by the Catholic Church?

1 It was towards the end of his life. Jesus was trying to prepare his disciples for his death. It was only a short time away. He said to Peter:

'I tell you, Peter, you are a rock and on this rock foundation I will build my Church, and not even death will be able to overcome it. I will give you the keys of the kingdom of heaven, what you prohibit on earth will be prohibited in heaven and what you permit on earth will be permitted in heaven.' (Matthew 16.18, 19)

Why do you think that these words have always been very important to Catholics?

2 What are the responsibilities of:

a the Pope?
b the Cardinals?
c the bishops?
d the parish priest?
e the deacons?

For your dictionary

Baptism is the service of initiation into the Christian Church.

The most important bishops in the Catholic Church are called **Cardinals**.

Confirmation is the service through which a person becomes a full member of the Christian Church. They can now take Holy Communion.

The **Mass** is the term used in the Roman Catholic Church for the service of Holy Communion.

A **sacrament** is a visible sign of God's inward blessing.

Simon Peter (the rock) was the fisherman who became a disciple of Jesus.

Why is the symbol of a bunch of keys associated with St Peter?

What is the Anglican Church?

If you lived in Britain and saw only one church in the whole of your lifetime the chances are that it would belong to the Church of England. This is because the Church of England has been the 'official' (Established) Church in this country since the time of Queen Elizabeth I. The Queen is its head and its leader is the **Archbishop of Canterbury**. Unlike the Pope, the Archbishop is just one bishop amongst many.

The Church of England is run by the General Synod, a kind of Church parliament. It is divided into three groups, or Houses: Bishops, Clergy and ordinary Church members, called Laity.

What is the Anglican Church?

There are now Churches all over the world which follow the teachings of the Church of England. They cannot, however, be called the Church of England or recognise the Queen as their head. These Churches belong to the Anglican Communion. Many of them are Episcopalian, for example the Episcopal Church in Scotland and the Episcopal Church in America, which means that the Church has bishops. Bishops are obviously important Church leaders but can you find out what their responsibilities are?

In many ways the Anglican Church and the Roman Catholic Church are similar. This is hardly surprising. For much of their history they have been part of the same Church. Since the break between them in the sixteenth century, though, the Church of England has also taken on board many Protestant ideas as well. In practice, this means that:

- many Anglican Churches are more Protestant than Roman Catholic. They are called Low Church or **Evangelical**.

- many Anglican Churches are more Roman Catholic than Protestant. They are called **Anglo-Catholic**.

If you go into an Anglican church you can easily tell whether it is Evangelical or Anglo-Catholic. Evangelical churches are plain and simple whilst Anglo-Catholic churches resemble Roman Catholic churches with candles, incense and, sometimes, statues of the Virgin Mary. These contrasts show how the Church of England has tried to balance its Protestant feelings with its Catholic traditions over the centuries.

Since it was formed the Church of England has lost many of its members who have left to form other Churches. The Methodist Church, in particular,

These photographs show the inside and outside of the same cathedral. Can you find out why the building is called a 'cathedral' and why it is different from other churches?

had its roots firmly in the Church of England. The break took place in the eighteenth century and in the 1970s discussions took place about reuniting the two Churches but nothing changed. The Congregationalists, who split away from the Church of England because they believed that each local church should have control over its own affairs, joined with the Presbyterians in 1972 to form the United Reform Church.

Which of these two Anglican buildings is Low Church and which is High Church? How can you tell?

- What is the difference between the Church of England and the Anglican Communion?
- Who is the Head of the Church of England?
- Who is the senior bishop in the Church of England?

 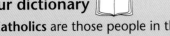
The Church of England is organised in this way:

The Queen
▼
The Archbishop of Canterbury
▼
The Archbishop of York

Bishops

Priests

Deacons

The local congregation

Can you find out:

a why the Church of England is called the 'Established Church'?

b three ways in which the Church of England is treated differently to other Churches in this country?

c the name of the body which runs the Church of England and which three groups are represented in it?

Who are the Protestants?

There are millions of Protestants in the world and thousands of different Protestant Churches. Do you know what a Protestant is? If not, look at the word closely. What other word does it suggest to you? Every 'Protestant' Church has grown out of protest of some kind.

Early Protestants

It all started in the sixteenth century with the Reformation. The two leadings lights of the time, Martin Luther (1483–1546) in Germany and John Calvin (1509–1564) in Switzerland were both Catholics who wanted to reform their own Church. They encouraged people to find new ways of worshipping God but they fell foul of their own Church leaders. Both of them set up their own Churches:

- the Lutheran Church, found mainly in German-speaking countries, Scandinavia and North America. There are now about 70 000 000 Lutherans. Their basic belief is that people are accepted by God through faith.

- the Calvinistic Churches which are mainly in Europe, North America and South Africa. The Presbyterian Church in Scotland is an important Calvinist Church. These Churches believe strongly that God has supreme power.

Try to find out three facts about Martin Luther.

What are the Free Churches?

During the seventeenth and eighteenth centuries many new Churches were born, known as Free or Nonconformist Churches. They 'freed' themselves from the Church of England. Amongst them were:

The Quakers
'Quakers' was the nickname given to members of the Society of Friends by a judge who was told by George Fox (1624–1691), their founder, 'to quake and fear at the word of the Lord.' Quaker worship is the simplest of all. Quakers have no **creed**, sacraments, priests or services. Instead, as they come together in a **meeting house**, they sit in silence unless someone feels called by God to speak.

The Baptists
With 32 000 000 members worldwide the **Baptist Church** is the largest Free Church. A Baptist Church can always be recognised by its use of **Believer's Baptism** – baptising only those people who are old enough to know what they are doing.

Why do you think that the Salvation Army was organised like an army from the beginning?

The Methodists

Methodists are a group founded in the eighteenth century by two brothers, John and Charles Wesley, who were both Anglican clergymen. In Methodist worship there is an emphasis on hymn singing, Bible reading and preaching.

The Salvation Army

William Booth (1829–1912) set up the **Salvation Army** in 1880 after working in slum areas. He founded his Army on military lines, with the minister being an officer and ordinary members the soldiers. You can tell their rank by the uniform they wear. The Salvation Army still works amongst the poorest and most needy in society at home and overseas.

There are many different Protestant Churches and we have only mentioned a very small sample of them. They are certainly very different from each other. Some have bishops whilst others do not. Most celebrate the sacraments of baptism and Holy Communion but the Salvation Army and Quakers do not have any sacraments. All, however, place the Bible at the centre of their preaching and emphasise that each person is responsible for their own faith.

- What does the word 'Protestant' mean?
- What are the Free Churches?
- Why are members of the Society of Friends called 'Quakers'?

For your dictionary

The **Baptist Church** is a worldwide Protestant denomination which only baptises adults.
In the Baptist Church's **Believer's Baptism**, only adults who are believers in Jesus Christ are baptised.
A **creed** is a statement of faith by the Church.
A **meeting house** is the place where Quakers come together for worship.
The **Methodists** came into being through the preaching of an Anglican clergyman, John Wesley.
The **Quakers** is a Christian denomination with its own very distinctive style of worship.
The **Salvation Army** was formed by William Booth to work in the poorest parts of Britain.

On whose teaching and inspiration is the Methodist Church based?

1 There are many different Protestant Churches. Draw up a chart like the one below and describe two distinctive characteristics of each Church.

Church	Characteristics
Baptists	1
	2
Methodists	1
	2
Salvation Army	1
	2
Quakers	1
	2

2 Seven names from this chapter are hidden in this wordsquare. The words can be written across or down. Find them and then write two sentences to explain each of them.

W	R	Y	U	O	D	A	G	H	K	L
C	T	Y	I	O	A	L	M	G	U	P
A	Q	W	C	V	L	U	T	H	E	R
L	V	B	O	Q	U	A	K	E	R	O
V	L	H	J	L	I	K	O	Y	N	T
I	B	V	X	Z	N	Y	T	R	U	E
N	W	N	I	F	M	L	O	P	U	S
M	E	T	H	O	D	I	S	T	Y	T
X	S	G	H	L	H	Y	U	I	K	A
M	L	Y	R	W	Q	B	H	F	S	N
T	E	B	A	P	T	I	S	T	G	T
M	Y	V	G	J	H	L	K	M	I	Y

Who are the Evangelicals?

The Evangelicals are not a Church. They are Christians who are found in most Christian denominations and who adopt a distinctive approach to their faith in God. They are the fastest growing group in the Church with 1 in 4 Christians claiming to be Evangelicals, 400 000 000 people in all.

What is an Evangelical?

An Evangelical Christian is someone who believes that:

- The Bible is the inspired Word of God and faultless from beginning to end. Anyone who wants to hear what God is trying to say to them must read and listen to the Bible.

- Each person needs to be converted before they can enter into a personal relationship with God through Jesus Christ.

- Every Christian has the responsibility to witness to others about their own faith in Christ. If you come across a group of people singing and preaching on a street corner or handing out religious leaflets the chances are that they will be Evangelicals.

Why do you think that Evangelical Christians feel an overwhelming need to witness to their faith?

Many Evangelicals worship in the old, traditional churches. Two recent movements, though, have swelled their numbers.

The Charismatic Movement

In the last 25 years or so there have been an increasing number of Christian groups which have been displaying a free, uninhibited approach to worship. These people belong to the Charismatic Movement which has greatly affected many Roman Catholic, Anglican and Free churches. The word 'charismatic' comes from a Greek word meaning 'gifts' and its use here refers to the special powers that some Christians believe they have been given by God's Holy Spirit. Amongst these special powers are:

- the power to heal.

- the power to prophesy about the future.

- the power to speak in unknown languages when praying which is called **speaking in tongues**.

In their worship **charismatics** express a great joy and depth of feeling about their faith. They often clap their hands, close their eyes and lift their hands in the air to symbolise reaching out to heaven. Their services tend to be long and are full of music and singing. Why do you think that charismatic worship has proved to be so popular in many branches of the Christian Church, especially amongst young people?

The House-Church Movement

Looking at the name, what do you think this might be? It started off with people worshipping in each other's homes. As the movement grew, halls, cinemas and other places were rented. Some 20 000 Christians now meet in this way every Sunday.

Why start a new Church? Surely there are more than enough already. You might think so but most of the House Churches began because many Christians felt unhappy with the traditional Churches. Can you work out what might have made them feel unhappy? They wanted a style of worship that was informal, lively and friendly. When they couldn't find that in any of the existing Churches they decided to set up fellowships of their own.

- What is an Evangelical?
- What is the Charismatic Movement?
- What are House Churches?

Vicky and Jon belong to the same House Church. They both tried ordinary churches but did not like them. As they are engaged they decided to write a joint comment about their House Church:

'We both joined the same House Church within a few weeks of each other. When we got talking we discovered that our reasons for joining a House Church were very similar. Neither of us found the worship in our previous churches satisfied us. It was too formal and predictable. We needed something that was more lively but also a form of worship with a strong teaching element. We needed to learn much more about the Bible and our own Christian faith. The House Church provided that.'

a Why do you think that Vicky and Jon left their own churches to join a House Church?
b Would you have done the same thing in similar circumstances?

WHAT WE BELIEVE

About God:
God is the Creator of all things. He is powerful, loving and pure, and He is one God in three Persons– Father, Son and Holy Spirit.

About Jesus Christ:
He is Gods Son, and is both fully human and fully divine. He died on the cross in the place of sinners, He rose again from the dead, He is alive today, and He will one day personally return to earth as the Judge of every person.

About the Holy Spirit:
He is fully divine and makes the work of Jesus Christ real in the lives of believers.

About Ourselves:

Which two beliefs does this particular Church hold?

Are the Churches moving closer together?

Have you any idea how many different churches there are in your area? It might be interesting to carry out a small survey to find out. Your research may make you wonder whether so many churches are really needed. How many people attend these churches on a Sunday? Wouldn't it make sense for some of the churches to pool their resources and combine with each other?

The ideal situation

Many Christians want to have closer links with fellow-believers from other churches. They believe that it is wrong for Christians to be separated from one another when they have so much in common. They remember that, on the night before he was betrayed, Jesus prayed that all his followers would be united:

'...that they may be one as you and I are one, Father.'
(John 17.11)

He went on to say that all his followers should be recognisable by the way that they love each other. What do you think this means? How might it apply to the many different churches?

The sad truth is that over the centuries Christians have argued, fought, disagreed and even killed one another. Today most of the world's Christians belong to one of three 'families' (Catholic, Anglican and Orthodox) which have only just begun speaking to one another after centuries of hostility. It remains to be seen whether they can go any further.

What is Church unity?

In 1910 representatives from the world's Protestant Churches met in Edinburgh for the World Missionary Conference. They had a problem because **missionaries** from the different Churches were competing against each other for converts. Then, in 1948, the **World Council of Churches** (WCC) was formed in Amsterdam. With 300 member Churches but without the Roman Catholic Church the WCC has spearheaded united Christian action across the world.

This was a big step towards Church unity. Another giant step was taken in 1960 when the Archbishop of Canterbury, Dr Geoffrey Fisher, visited Pope John XXIII in Rome. Until then the Catholic Church had kept itself very much to itself. Now there was a more open relationship with other Churches. This was cemented in 1984 when the present Pope, John Paul II, visited Canterbury to meet the Archbishop. For a time there was great enthusiasm for Church unity. Roman Catholic and Anglican leaders began to meet to discuss the issues that separated the two Churches. So far, though, nothing has actually been done. In fact, many people would say that things have gone backwards rather than forwards in recent years. Rather than wait for something dramatic to happen individual Christians from different Churches have begun to work together to tackle such problems as poverty, famine and homelessness. Perhaps this is the only practical way forward towards Church unity?

This is the symbol of the World Council of Churches. What does this symbol of a cross in a boat tell you about the aims of the movement?

Rather than wait for their Church leaders to agree on unity many Christians have united in helping the community, like this sheltered accommodation project for old people in Bath. Why do you think that Christians find it easy to unite in projects like this?

- Why did 1200 people meet at Edinburgh in 1910?
- Who visited the Pope in Rome in 1960 and why was this visit particularly important?
- How do Christians from different Churches work together today?

For your dictionary

A **missionary** is a person who is sent to tell people about God. The **World Council of Churches** links together many of the Churches of the world.

1 Paul was the most important leader in the early Christian Church. Here are two quotations from him. Read them carefully.

'There is no difference between the Jew and the Gentile, between slaves and free men, between men and women. You are all united because you believe in Jesus Christ.' (Galatians 3.28)

'Agree in everything you do so that there will not be any divisions among you.' (1 Corinthians 10.23)

a What do these two verses suggest about any disagreements that may exist between Christians?
b Paul was clearly upset by divisions in the Church of his day. Can you think of two issues that might split Christians today? Find out as much as you can about one of them.

2 Find out whether there is a local Council of Churches in your area. If so, invite a representative to your school to answer your questions. In particular, try to discover:

a What is a Council of Churches?
b Which Churches belong to the Council and which do not.
c How, and why, the Council was formed.
d What kind of work the Council does in your area.

What is Christian worship?

Whether they meet in a church building, in the open air or gather together in each other's homes, Christians meet regularly to worship God and pray with one another. The pattern of worship that they follow is very varied. This is not only true between one Church and another but even between members of the same Church. What are the advantages and disadvantages of having so much variety in Christian worship?

According to the book

Broadly speaking, you can divide Christian worship into two groups:

1   Most Churches have a service book in which the pattern for their worship is written down. The Anglican Church calls their prayer book the **Book of Common Prayer**, or, in the modern version, the **Alternative Service Book**. Roman Catholics have the **Missal** whilst in the Orthodox Church the order of service is the Divine Liturgy.

    Worship based upon a prayer book is elaborate, colourful and full of ritual. Even before the service begins many worshippers bow before the altar and make the sign of the cross over their bodies. These symbolic actions suggest an attitude and state of mind that the worshipper is adopting. Can you suggest what this is? In the service that follows hymns, chanting (a special kind of singing), prayers, Bible readings and a **sermon** are the main ingredients. With a little practice anyone can follow liturgical worship in their prayer book.

2   Many Churches have moved away from having a set pattern to their services. They have cut down on the rituals or eliminated them altogether. Instead they place the emphasis upon singing, personal testimonies, prayers and sermons. This kind of worship is most common in Protestant and Free Churches.

How important is Sunday?

Although there are meetings in most churches on other days **Sunday** is the main day for Christian worship. This day, the Lord's Day, is the day on which Jesus rose from the dead. Christians like to spend as much of it as possible worshipping God and resting from their normal activities. Do you think that the idea of having one day a week as a special day is important, whether or not you go to church on that day?

Why worship?

We have already spoken of Christian worship. What do Christians gain from the times that they come together to worship God? Through times of worship people:

- are encouraged to have feelings of praise, thanks-giving, joy, wonder and commitment to God. These feelings are expressed through silence, singing, clapping, dancing, praying, incense-burning, candle-lighting, reciting the creeds, reading the Bible and many other activities.

What do you think that people might hope to gain from going to a Church service on Sunday?

Is there something that Christians worshipping God in the open air might find which would not be present in a church?

- are given the opportunity to be forgiven and to forgive others.

- are inspired and strengthened to live as Christians in their daily lives.

Christians do not just worship God in church. They also do so in their daily lives. Their regular prayers and other personal devotions bring them into contact with God. They find God by helping and serving others. They experience God through the beauties of creation and nature. All of these things are true yet, for most Christians, going to church will always occupy an important place in their lives.

- On which day of the week do Christians meet together to worship God, and why?
- What are prayer or service books?
- Why do Christians worship God?

[1] Here is a questionnaire about Christian worship. Copy it into your exercise book and fill in the answers.

> **a** Why is Sunday an important day for Christians? Give two reasons.
> 1
> 2
> **b** Suggest two ways in which Christians might worship God individually.
> 1
> 2
> **c** Give two reasons for the variety in worship between the different Churches.
> 1
> 2
> **d** Christian worship involves serving other people. Find out three ways in which Christians serve other people today.
> 1
> 2
> 3

[2] Bishop Desmond Tutu, the Archbishop of Cape Town in South Africa, is one of the best-known modern Church leaders. Here are two things that he has said about Christian worship:

'We all have the need to worship.'

'True Christian worship can never let us be indifferent to the needs of others, to the cries of the hungry, of the naked and homeless, of the sick and the prisoners, of the oppressed and the disadvantaged.'

Read these quotations carefully. Put the words of Archbishop Tutu into your own words to show that you understand what he is saying.

What do Christians do?

The Church is made up of many people. It is found in almost every country of the world. Its members are from many different cultures and backgrounds. Each of them is trying to live out the command of Christ that they should:

'Love God…and love your neighbour as much as yourself.' (Mark 12.30, 31)

What do Christians do?

Amongst other things Christians:

- go to church. Most Christians try to attend one of their local churches each Sunday to meet with other Christians and to worship God.

- pray. Most Christians pray to God every day and they set aside a regular time for this. Sometimes they pray with others, sometimes they pray alone. Usually a Christian kneels and closes his or her eyes when praying. Can you suggest any reason for this?

- read the Bible. The Bible is the book which tells Christians about God, Jesus and themselves. Often Christians use notes which help them to understand the passage they are reading. There are very few Christians in the world who do not have at least part of the Bible in their own language now.

- teach others. Christians teach their children about Jesus and the Bible. They do this at home and also in Sunday Schools or Junior Churches which are attached to most churches.

- help others. Christians are responsible for running hostels for the homeless; feeding the hungry; contacting those who have run away from home; working amongst alcoholics and drug addicts etc. Money is collected at most church services and much of this goes to help the needy.

- work for peace and justice in the world. Some groups, especially the Quakers, are in the forefront of those working for peace and justice. Some of these Christians are **pacifists** and do not believe in war or violence.

Some Christians become full-time ministers in the Church although some Churches only allow men to do this. Others decide to become missionaries serving God at home or overseas. A few Christians enter a community of monks or nuns. Many do paid or unpaid work for Christian organisations.

- Which command of Jesus are Christians trying to live out in their everyday lives?
- What is a pacifist?
- Which groups of needy people in our society do Christians try to help?

For your dictionary 📖
A **pacifist** is someone who will not fight in a war or use violence.

Why do you think that this regular church meeting plays an important role in the lives of these old people?

These drawings show five activities which most Christians do.
Produce your own drawings and write two sentences underneath
each one to explain what is happening.

What kind of problems would you expect this London City Missioner to
meet on the streets of London?

What is church like?

Christians have been building churches in which to worship God since the third century. Until then they had been worshipping in each other's houses but there were now too many of them to continue doing this. It seemed to make sense to set aside special buildings for worship. From the very beginning the design and furniture of these buildings were carefully made to help those inside them worship God.

A traditional English church

Take an example with which many of us are reasonably familiar: the old, traditional English parish church. Some of those that are still standing date from the twelfth century, making them over 800 years old. Open the door, step inside and you will find your eyes drawn to the altar at the far end of the building. Stay for a service of Holy Communion and you will see Christians going forward to the altar to receive the bread and wine. For those who originally built the church the altar represented the final goal in life, the place only reached at death. Both the service and the building combine to be symbols, to light the way of each worshipper through life to death.

Many of these early buildings were built in the shape of a cross. Can you think of any reason for this? Do you know of any symbols which you might find inside a church? Have you worked out what these symbols mean?

Do you have a parish church close to you? If so, pay it a visit to find out about its design and history. Write up any information that you find in your exercise book.

What are the most noticeable differences between this new cathedral and the much older abbey shown on page 10?

Ancient and modern churches

By putting the altar at the far end of the building the builders wanted to make God seem far away – remote but holy. The same idea is conveyed in an Orthodox church by a screen, covered with icons or holy pictures, which hides the altar from the sight of ordinary worshippers.

Churches built in recent times are very different. Instead of putting the altar as far away from the people as possible it is placed in the middle of the congregation. Seats are then gathered around the altar in a circle or semi-circle. The priest stands among the people as he conducts the service instead of being separate from them. What do you think is the meaning of all these changes?

In fact, some modern churches are circular in shape. This allows everyone to feel that they are part of what is going on. As a result there is a more friendly atmosphere. One example of this is Clifton Cathedral in Bristol. The people who worship there regularly say that its shape and design help them to feel that God is with his people.

Free Churches

Just as the altar is the focal point in most Anglican and Catholic churches so the **pulpit** commands your attention as you enter a Free Church. This is not a coincidence. The service of Holy

Communion, conducted at the altar, is the centre of Anglican and Catholic worship and the preaching of God's Word, the Bible, is the most important ingredient in Free Church worship. Otherwise the buildings are simple, often containing little more than a cross. Many Christians feel that the building in which they worship God should contain as few distractions as possible. Do you agree?

Most Free Church religious buildings are called **chapels** although members of the Salvation Army meet together in a **citadel**.

- What is the altar in a church?
- What acts as the focal point in a Free Church building?
- Why is there a screen at the front of an Orthodox church?

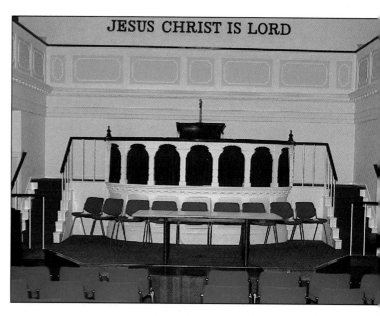
JESUS CHRIST IS LORD

What features can you pick out in this Free Church building?

1 Arrange a visit to a local church and use a questionnaire similar to the one below to find out some important information.

Name of church:

Denomination:

What services are held every week?

Are there meetings other than those in church?
Give examples.

Are there child/youth activities?
Give examples.

How is the church involved with the community?

Number of full-time workers:

Then use the results of your research to answer these questions:
a What do you think is at the centre of this church's life?
b How active is the church amongst children and young people?

c How many full-time workers are supported by the church?
d Which activities do you think might appeal to:
an elderly person living on his own?
a young mother with a baby?
a married couple?
a teenage brother and sister?

2 When the Christian Church first began there were no buildings. The Church was then only about people. Look up each of the following references in the Bible and summarise, on a chart like this, what they tell us about the early Christian Church.

Reference	Information
Acts 2.43–47	1.
	2.
	3.
Acts 2.12–16.	1.
	2.
	3.
Acts 4.32–38.	1.
	2.
	3.

For your dictionary
A **chapel** is a Free Church place of worship.
A Salvation Army place of worship is called a **citadel**.
A **pulpit** is the raised platform from which a sermon is delivered in church.

What are church services like?

Have you been to a church service recently? If so, which church did you go to? Perhaps you have been to more than one type of church? If so, you will know that church services can come in many different shapes and sizes. In this chapter we are going to look at two different kinds of service.

The Quakers

You could not imagine a simpler form of Christian worship than that of the Society of Friends or Quakers. Friends come together in a very simple and plain building called a meeting house with no priest or minister to lead them in worship. Instead two of their number, a man and a woman, preside over the service.

As the people arrive on a Sunday morning they sit together in a circle in silence. The silence is only broken if and when someone feels inspired by the Holy Spirit to speak. Someone may then feel inspired to respond to what has been said or the silence will be allowed to resume. No one is under any pressure at all to open their mouths.

As you can imagine the atmosphere in a Quaker meeting is one of quiet and calm. This form of worship stems from the Quaker belief that it is up to each person to establish their own relationship with God. Everyone must wait for the still, small voice of God to speak and human words often get in the way. It is all very different from the powerful singing and music of the Baptists, Methodists and Salvation Army.

The Free Churches

Like the Quakers, Free Church worship is kept as simple as possible but it is more organised. Little time is given to ceremony and ritual but a great emphasis is laid upon the Bible and its teachings. If the service is one of Holy Communion then it is likely to follow a set pattern but otherwise it is unlikely to be planned in detail. The main ingredients are likely to be:

- singing. Some of the greatest Christian hymns have come from the Free Churches, especially the Methodist Church.

- prayers. Whilst some of these are written down the majority are extempore, which means the person praying says what comes into his or her mind at the time. The Lord's Prayer is said at almost all services.

- Bible readings. At least two are included and one will normally form the basis of the sermon.

- preaching. This is the climax to a Free Church service.

Within this framework the people are often free to express themselves. Some people may clap their hands, others may call out 'Yes, Lord' and 'Hallelujah' when someone says something they agree with. In this way they feel they are a part of the service.

What do you think is the real value of silence in Christian worship?

- Which group of Christians hope to hear the still, small voice of God through their worship?
- What is most unusual about a Quaker service?
- What is the most important feature of worship in a Free Church?

These Christians are waving their arms as part of a Christian service. Why do you think they are doing this?

1 Prepare your own questionnaire to find out which kind of church services people prefer and why. Include older people in your survey to balance the opinions of young people. Remember to find out how many of the people that you interview go to church and why some do not.

2 John and Anne are both Christians but they go to very different places of worship. John is a Quaker who attends a meeting house in the nearest town whilst Anne goes to a Free Church. This is what the two of them have to say about worship:

Anne, 25

'I really look forward to my hour of peace and quiet every Sunday morning. I live a very hectic life and it is wonderful just to get off the crazy merry-go-round, stop, think and listen to God's Spirit.'

John, 22

'I like my Church services to have real life and urgency in them. I enjoy singing some of the old hymns but I really like some of the new Christian music. It really goes with a swing. I like to dance in services as well because that is the best way for me to express my Christian faith.'

If you were thinking of joining a church which of these two styles of worship would most appeal to you? Can you explain why?

What is Christian prayer?

More than 80 per cent of us pray when we are really in trouble. Only about 10 per cent of us pray when life is going well. Most Christians, of course, would be amongst the 10 per cent! They believe that praying is one of the most important of all activities and not only when they are in a tight spot. They try to pray each day, both with other people and also on their own.

Whilst most Christians do make up their own prayers many of them also like to use prayers put together by other people. The prayer which is used most by all Christians is the Lord's Prayer.

What is a rosary?

What's in a prayer?

Christians believe that they are closest to God when they are praying. Sometimes they repeat the words set down in a prayer book or, as in the case of Catholic Christians, make frequent use of a **rosary**. A rosary is a set of beads and each part reminds the worshipper of an event, or 'mystery', in the life of Jesus. The **Hail Mary**, a formal prayer, is said ten times and the Lord's Prayer, called the 'Our Father', once.

Most prayers are not completely haphazard. They follow common themes. Amongst the most important of these are:

- Adoration – thanking God for his greatness and power.

- Confession – the feeling that, when confronted by the greatness of God, the only appropriate response is to be aware of one's own sinfulness. A confession of sin is always followed by an awareness of forgiveness.

- Intercession – speaking to God on someone else's behalf. Through praying Christians try to become more aware of the needs of others so they pray for the hungry, the poor, the lonely, the homeless and other people in need. Which groups of needy people in today's world do you think might figure prominently in a Christian's prayers?

- Petition – asking God for something.

- Thanksgiving – a form of prayer which expresses a person's thanks to God.

Look at the Lord's Prayer in Exercise 1. Can you find each of these different elements in that prayer?

Is there a go-between?

Most Christian prayers are addressed to God directly and end with the words 'Through Jesus Christ, our Lord'. This is because Christians believe that God is too great to be addressed directly and so they need a go-between or mediator. That mediator is Jesus. Roman Catholics believe that prayers can also be addressed to God through Mary, the mother of Jesus.

What is meditation?

Christians do not all pray in the same way. Many of them kneel to pray and put their hands together whilst others stand or sit. Some make the sign of the cross on their bodies to remind themselves of the crucifixion of Jesus. Some pray at set times, for example, in the morning and last thing at night, whilst others pray when the mood takes them.

Some Christians use words when they pray but others do not. **Meditation** is a quiet form of praying where the worshipper seeks to concentrate his or her mind upon God. Some Christians meditate a great deal and some religious orders of monks and nuns are called contemplative which means that they see praying as their main reason for existing.

Why do you think that it is traditional for Christians to kneel and close their eyes when they are praying? Why do you think that most of us pray at some time or other?

- What is intercession?
- What is meditation?
- What does a contemplative order of monks or nuns specialise in?

For your dictionary

The **Hail Mary** is a favourite prayer of Roman Catholics. It is based on the words of the Angel Gabriel when he told Mary that she was to have a baby.

Meditation is a form of prayer found in many religions.

A **rosary** is a string of beads which Roman Catholics use to help them meditate on the lives of Jesus and the Virgin Mary.

1 According to Matthew and Luke, Jesus taught his disciples to pray by giving them a model prayer. As you will see there are some differences in the two versions:

'Our father who art in heaven,
Hallowed be your name.
Your Kingdom come,
Your will be done on earth as it is in heaven.
Give us this day our daily bread;
And forgive us our debts,
As we also have forgiven our debtors;
And lead us not into temptation,
But deliver us from evil…'
(Matthew 6.9–13)

'Father,
Hallowed be your name,
Your Kingdom come,
Give us each day our daily bread;
And forgive us our sins,
for we also forgive everyone who is indebted to us;
and lead us not into temptation.'
(Luke 11.2–4)

Today most English-speaking Christians use a mixture of these two versions. Write out the version of the prayer that you know. Work out whether each phrase was taken from Matthew's or Luke's version.

2 Here are two very popular Christian prayers:

The Evening Collect, used in Anglican churches:

'Lighten our darkness we beseech thee, O Lord;
And by thy great mercy, defend us from all the perils and dangers of this night,
For the love of thy only Son, our Saviour, Jesus Christ.'

The Jesus Prayer, used by Orthodox Christians:

'Lord Jesus Christ, Son of God, have mercy on me a sinner.'

a Why do Christians find that the Evening Collect is a suitable prayer for the end of the day?
b Why do you think that many Orthodox Christians repeat the Jesus Prayer over and over again?
c Find out why most Christian prayers end with the word 'Amen'.

How are Christians helped to pray?

Many Christians, mainly Protestants, do not make use of anything to help them to pray, apart from the Bible. Christians from Roman Catholic and Orthodox backgrounds find that a rosary, an icon or a crucifix are useful when they say their prayers.

What is a rosary?

There are many individual Christians, from different denominations, who use a rosary when they are praying. A rosary is a string of beads made up of five groups of ten beads. Each single bead marks the divisions between the groups of beads. Attached to one of the single beads is a group of three beads, another single bead and a crucifix.

Each group of beads has a distinctive feel to it so that the worshipper can pass them through the fingers without needing to look at them. In working their way through the rosary each worshipper says three different prayers:

- the Lord's Prayer (called the Our Father or Pater Noster).

- the Hail Mary (also called the Ave Maria).

- the Gloria Patri.

Altogether there are 15 holy mysteries which the worshipper is expected to think about as he or she says the rosary. In practice, though, the person is only likely to contemplate one group of five mysteries. They are:

- the five joyful mysteries connected with the birth of Jesus.

- the five sorrowful mysteries connected with the death of Jesus.

- the five glorious mysteries connected with the resurrection of Jesus and the taking up of Mary into heaven.

Why do you think that many Christians find contemplation like this useful?

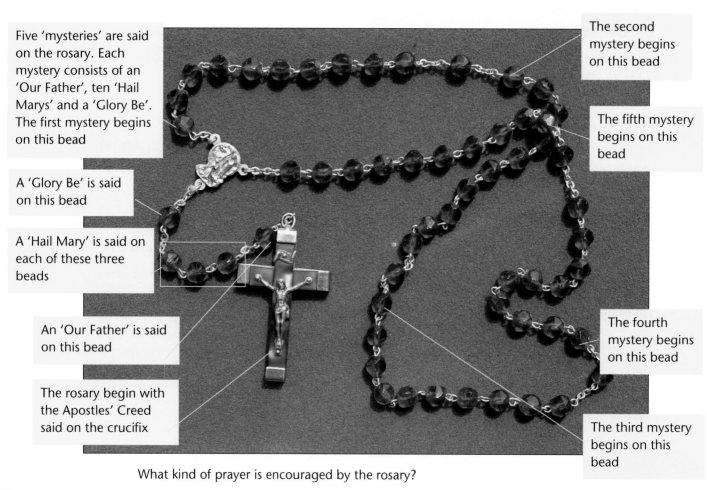

Five 'mysteries' are said on the rosary. Each mystery consists of an 'Our Father', ten 'Hail Marys' and a 'Glory Be'. The first mystery begins on this bead

A 'Glory Be' is said on this bead

A 'Hail Mary' is said on each of these three beads

An 'Our Father' is said on this bead

The rosary begin with the Apostles' Creed said on the crucifix

The second mystery begins on this bead

The fifth mystery begins on this bead

The fourth mystery begins on this bead

The third mystery begins on this bead

What kind of prayer is encouraged by the rosary?

Why do you think that many Christians need this constant reminder of the death of Jesus?

What is a crucifix?

A crucifix is a cross with an image of Jesus on it. You will find them in many churches or hanging around people's necks. A crucifix is often given as a present to mark an event such as a confirmation.

Many people use a crucifix to remember the sufferings of Jesus. Some Christians say that they find it very moving to pray in front of a crucifix. Often the initials INRI are to be seen on the crucifix above the head of Jesus. These letters stand for 'Jesus of Nazareth, King of the Jews' from the Latin words 'Iesus Nazarenus Rex Iudaeorum'.

What is an icon?

An icon is a religious picture of Jesus, Mary or one of the saints. It is usually painted on wood although other materials can be used. Icons are most popular in Orthodox churches where they form an important part of religious worship. They are often kissed and have candles lit in front of them as a sign of respect.

Why are icons important? Many Christians believe that saints can exercise their power today through these religious paintings. Some of the saints have even become well-known for the healings that are said to have come about because of them. Yet when a worshipper is offering a prayer in front of an icon they are not praying to the painting itself. They are using the icon as a means of directing their prayer towards God.

These two prayers are recited whenever a rosary is used:

The Hail Mary
Hail, Mary, full of grace,
The Lord is with you.
Blessed are you among women and blessed is the fruit of your womb, Jesus.
Holy Mary, Mother of God,
Pray for us sinners now
And at the hour of our death. Amen.

The Gloria Patri
Glory be to the Father and to the Son and to the Holy Spirit. As it was in the beginning, is now and ever shall be, world without end. Amen.

a The Hail Mary says several things about Mary, the mother of God. What are they?
b Why do you think that the Gloria Patri is said several times during the rosary?

- What is a crucifix?
- How do some Christians use a crucifix?
- What are the Hail Mary and the Gloria Patri?

What are icons and what part do they play in the private devotions of many Christians?

Who are the Church leaders?

You may remember an incident from the life of Jesus in which he began to wash the feet of his disciples. When Peter protested that this was normally the work of the lowest servant in the household Jesus replied:

'You call me Master and Lord and rightly; so I am. If I, then, the Lord and Master, have washed your feet, you should wash other people's feet. I have given you an example so that you can copy what I have done for you.' (John 13.14, 15)

By doing this Jesus was setting an example to everyone who would be a Christian leader. They are reminded that their main task is to serve others.

Servants within the Church

Many Free Churches recognise this idea of service when they call their leaders **ministers**. The same idea is carried by the Baptists who prefer to call their leaders **pastors** – shepherds of the flock. Roman Catholic, Anglican and Orthodox Churches use the word 'priest'. Can you find out what it means?

A bishop is a senior priest who is given overall responsibility for the churches in his area. Both the Anglican and Catholic Churches have bishops. In the Orthodox Church the senior priests are called **patriarchs** which means great fathers.

Below the bishop stands the parish priest. For anyone who wishes to be a priest there is a long period of training. In the case of Roman Catholic priests it is six years. At the end of this time they are ordained into the priesthood. This simply means that a bishop lays his hands upon their heads so that they can receive God's Holy Spirit. From now on they can conduct all services and celebrate the sacraments. In 1994 women were allowed to become priests for the first time in the Church of England.

What is a priest?

In the Orthodox and Roman Catholic Churches the priest is believed to represent the people to God and to be God's representative to the people. This is why at the very important services of the Mass and the Divine Liturgy the bread and wine become the body and blood of Christ through the priest. He is that important.

Many Protestant Churches, however, see things differently. To them the priest is simply the person who leads the church members in worship. They believe that God speaks to them through the Holy Spirit using the words of the Bible. What the minister has to say is very important but what really matters to them is what God has to say through the Bible.

For your dictionary

Within the Free Churches, the leader of a church is usually called a **minister**.
Baptist Churches prefer to call their church leaders **pastors**.
In the Orthodox Churches bishops are called **patriarchs**.

- Why do Free Churches call their leaders ministers or pastors?
- What is ordination?
- What is a bishop?

1 Look carefully at these photographs showing a Church of England vicar (left), a Roman Catholic priest (top right) and a Free Church minister.

a What is distinctive about what each of them is wearing?
b What does the appearance of each tell us about the tradition they represent?
c What do all three have in common? (Clue: What can you see in all three pictures?)

2 This page is taken from the diary of an Anglican vicar. It shows a typical week in his life. He is responsible for two churches: St Philip's and St Mark's.

19 MONDAY
Day off – go out!

20 TUESDAY
9.00–10.45 Dictate letters to Church secretary.
11.00 Funeral.
1.00–2.00 Quiet time.

21 WEDNESDAY
9.00 School assembly.
12.00–1.00 Golden Oldies Lunch Club.
1.00–2.00 Quiet time.
7.30 Parochial Church Council meeting.

22 THURSDAY
9.00–12.00 Working with Church secretary.
1.00–2.00 Quiet time.
2.30 Funeral.
3.30 Hospital visiting.
7.30 Men's meeting.
10.30 Soup run to homeless.

23 FRIDAY
9.00–12.00 Sermon preparation.
7.30 Church Bible study/prayer meeting.

24 SATURDAY
8.00 Church prayer meeting.
12.00 Church fête.
2.30 Wedding.
7.30 Choir rehearsal.

25 SUNDAY
8.00 Holy Communion (St Mark's).
10.00 Family Communion.
11.30 Morning Prayer (St Mark's).
4.00 Infant baptism.
6.30 Evening service (St Philip's).
8.30 Young people's evening.

How would you describe a typical week in the life of a vicar? Does it appeal to you as a job? What kind of activities do you think bring a vicar most satisfaction?

3 The Ordination Service speaks of the duties of a priest like this:

'…a priest is called by God to work…as servant and shepherd among the people…to proclaim the word of the Lord…to declare the forgiveness of sins…to baptise…to preside at the celebration of Holy Communion…to lead his people in prayer and worship…to minister to the sick, to prepare the dying for their death…'

Try to explain what you think each of these phrases means:
a '…as servant and shepherd among the people.'
b '…to proclaim the word of the Lord.'
c '…to minister to the sick.'
d '…to prepare the dying for their death.'

Do actions speak louder than words?

We often express the way that we are feeling by the movements of our bodies or the actions we perform, even if we are not aware of it at the time! You do not need to be told that someone is happy when you see them jumping up and down with excitement or that something is wrong with a friend when you see the miserable look on their face.

Actions in Christian worship

In Christian worship, too, people express their feelings about God by the way in which they behave or the actions they perform. Remember, though, it is always the meaning behind the action and not the action itself which is important. Think about these examples which have been drawn from many different kinds of Christian worship:

- As they enter church some people bow to the cross on the altar at the front, make the sign of the cross on their bodies or bow down on one knee (an action called **genuflecting**). The sign of the cross is an important Christian action and you will often see the Pope, a bishop or a priest make the sign over a whole congregation of people. Used in this way it is a form of blessing.

- Praying is a basic Christian activity but how does the worshipper use his or her body to express how they feel about God? In most churches worshippers kneel or bow their heads and close their eyes when they are praying. In this way, each person is expressing the respect that they have for God (bowing their head) and trying to shut out all distractions as they pray (closing their eyes). They are also saying something about themselves. Can you work out what it is?

- Other Christians, usually charismatics, extend their arms upward as they pray or sing. This suggests feelings of happiness and surrender to God. It also indicates that the person is ready and open to receive all that God has to give them. When you open your arms to someone you show them that you are pleased to see them!

- Touching is also an important part of Christian worship. In many Holy Communion services there is a part, called the Peace, where people kiss or shake hands with one another. As they do so they say 'Peace be with you'. They are expressing the warmth of Christian friendship based on the belief that all Christians are brothers and sisters and members of the same family.

Actions are an essential ingredient in Christian worship. If you think about it, you can probably come up with many other examples that we have not mentioned.

What do you think this particular symbolic action signifies?

Can you explain why this person has shut his eyes as he prays?

- How do most Christians show respect for God when they pray?
- What is genuflecting?
- What is 'the Peace' in Christian worship?

For your dictionary

When a person is **genuflecting** they kneel briefly on their right knee in front of the altar.

1 Use the words in bold type to fill in the blanks in this paragraph:

Often, on going into a _____ , a person will bow their knee or _____ . They might also make the _____ _____ _____ _____ in front of the _____ . Often they lift up their _____ when they are praying.

altar church genuflect sign of the cross hands

2 Answer each of these questions in just one sentence.

a   What do some people do as they enter a church?
b   What is the sign of the cross?
c   What are people doing when they bow their heads and close their eyes as they pray?
d   Why do some Christians lift their hands and eyes to heaven as they pray?
e   What is 'the Peace'?

3 In this table six common actions performed in Christian prayers are described. Copy the table into your exercise book. Say why each action is performed.

Action	Why is it performed?
Hands are put together.	
Genuflecting.	
Eyes are closed.	
People kiss.	
The sign of the cross.	
People pray on their knees.	

Why are symbols used in Christian worship?

One of the first things that strike you as you go into a church is the number of pictures and objects which carry a symbolic meaning. They are there to help people to worship God. A symbol is something which represents something else which is difficult to put into words.

Why use symbols?

There are two main reasons why Christians use symbols in their religious worship:

- A religious faith is difficult to explain at the best of times. Often, symbols are the only way to make it intelligible. Take, for example, the **halo** (circle) which you have probably seen in paintings above the heads of Jesus and the saints. At first glance this may look strange, but it is intended to send you a message about the person concerned. Do you know what the message is?

- Symbols help people to express the way that they feel about God. Incense and flowers, for example, are frequently to be found in churches but do you know what they symbolise?

Colours and symbols

Christians often use colours as symbols. They frequently decorate their church in white, for example – the colour which symbolises purity – when they want to celebrate a triumphant event in the life of Jesus. On **Easter Sunday**, when they remember the rising of Jesus from the dead, white and yellow are the dominant colours in church. Two days earlier, however, on **Good Friday** the dominant colours are black or purple, as Christians remember the death of Jesus on the cross. Seven weeks later, at **Pentecost**, the church is decorated in red as a reminder of the gift of the Holy Spirit as 'fiery flames' to the early Christians.

Clothes and symbols

Clothes play an important part in the life of the church. Take, for example, the clerical or dog collar worn by most priests and ministers. Why do they wear it? It has nothing to do with dogs but resembles the halter which was placed around the necks of slaves to prevent them from escaping. Why do you think that this is an appropriate form of dress for a priest to wear?

Some nuns still wear a traditional habit. The veil and the long dress are symbols of their modesty. The habit is in a plain colour to show that she has no material possessions of her own. The belt around her waist is tied with three knots as a reminder of the three-fold vow she took when she became a nun. She promised to:

- live a life of poverty.

- live a life of obedience to God.

- live a life of chastity. She is reminded of this particular vow by the ring that she wears on her left hand to show that she is married to God and to the Church.

Think hard and you will, no doubt, be able to add many more examples of symbols to the list.

- What is a symbol?
- Which colours are important Christian symbols and what do they symbolise?
- Which items of clothing are important Christian symbols?

Can you think of a modern symbol which might be used today to express the same message as this halo?

In this photograph you can see the symbols of incense and flowers in a church service. Can you think of any other symbols which might be visible?

1 Many Christians find that symbols help them in their worship. Here are three symbols which are used widely:

Some churches have candles on their altars. Light suggests the presence of God.

A crucifix is a reminder to worshippers of the death of Jesus.

Some churches have statues of Jesus or Mary. These set an example for all worshippers to follow.

Copy and complete this table in your exercise book.

Symbol	Meaning
Lighting candles	
Statue of Mary	
Crucifix	

2 As you can see, the badge worn by a Salvation Army officer is full of symbolism. Many of those symbols are indicated in this picture. Can you find out what each of them mean?

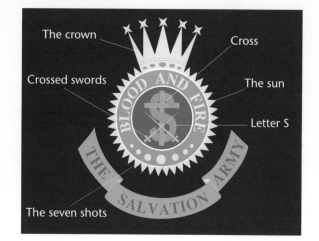

The crown
Cross
Crossed swords
The sun
Letter S
The seven shots

What is Holy Communion?

The central act of Christian worship is Holy Communion. But each Church has its own preferred name for this service and each name conveys a different way of understanding. We will look at the Roman Catholic Mass and the Orthodox Divine Liturgy later. Here we visit a Holy Communion service, or the **Eucharist**, as it is practised by the Anglican Church.

How did Holy Communion begin?

Meals are a very important part of family life. They are often times when members of the family talk and share things together.

On the night before he was betrayed by Judas Iscariot Jesus shared a meal with his disciples. It was to be the last meal that they were to share together before his death, although the disciples did not know this at the time. It was a meal to celebrate the Jewish festival of **Pesach** (Passover). After they had eaten together Jesus did something rather special. You can read Matthew's account in Exercise 1. Jesus also told his disciples to continue to break bread together as a memorial to him. What do you think he meant by this? As soon as he left the earth the disciples started to meet together to 'break bread'. They continue to do so today. The service is called Holy Communion.

What can we learn from this banner about Holy Communion?

What happens in Holy Communion?

There are two parts to the Anglican service of Holy Communion:

The ministry of the Word

During the first part of the service the Bible is read, a sermon is preached and prayers are said. In these each worshipper seeks God's forgiveness for his or her own sins (called the **confession** and **absolution**) and remembers the needs of others (called **intercession**). In many Eucharistic services a creed (a statement of belief) is then recited by everyone.

The ministry of the Sacrament

The worshippers give each other the kiss of peace as the service moves towards its climax, to show that they are all brothers and sisters in Christ. Then the words and actions of Jesus at the Last Supper are repeated and the bread and wine are given to the worshippers as they kneel at the altar rail.

What does Holy Communion mean?

What did Jesus mean when he said to the disciples that the bread was his body and the wine his blood? After all, when he said those words he was sitting, alive and well, in front of them. He was obviously looking into the immediate future. Within hours his body would be nailed to a cross. So, what does happen when Christians eat the bread and drink the wine?

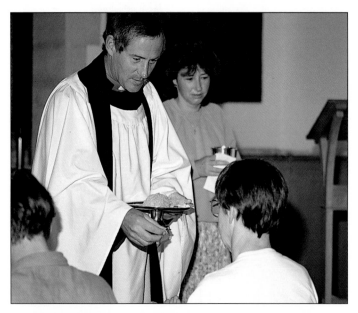

Why do you think that this service is called Holy Communion?

- Many Anglicans, along with many Christians in the Free Churches, believe that the Eucharist is a time for remembering and being thankful for the death of Jesus. During the service, therefore, the bread and wine remain what they are – bread and wine.
- Other Anglicans, along with Roman Catholics, believe that at some time during Holy Communion the bread and wine are mysteriously changed into the body and blood of Jesus.

In most Anglican churches Holy Communion is now a family service celebrated on Sunday mornings. Although children cannot receive the bread and wine they are often taken forward to the altar rail to receive a special blessing from the priest.

- Why do Christians celebrate Holy Communion?
- What is the ministry of the Word?
- What is the ministry of the Sacrament?

For your dictionary

Absolution is the pronouncement by a priest that a person has been forgiven for their sins.
Confession is the acknowledgement of a person's sin to a priest.
Eucharist (meaning 'thanksgiving') is the name given by most Anglicans to the service of Holy Communion.
Intercession takes place when someone prays for someone else.
Pesach (Passover) is the Jewish festival recalling the release of the Jews from slavery in Egypt.

1 We read this in Matthew 26.26–28:

'While they were eating, Jesus took bread, gave thanks and broke it and gave to his disciples saying:
"Take and eat; this is my body."
Then he took the cup, gave thanks and offered it to them saying:
"Drink from it, all of you. This is the blood of the covenant which is poured out for many for the forgiveness of sins."'

a What did Jesus do before he gave the bread and wine to his disciples?
b What did Jesus say about the bread and wine? What do you think he meant?

2 Many Christians find a special joy in worshipping God in the Eucharist. Here are two Christians describing what the service means to them:

Jane, 24

'I have been a Christian for only a few months and I did not know what to expect when I first went to Holy Communion. From the beginning, I found it to be very special. It is a time of real quiet when I can think of Jesus and his love for me.'

Andrew, 18

'I am an Anglican but I believe, like Roman Catholics, that, in some mysterious way, the bread and wine become the body and blood of Jesus. I do not profess to understand what I am saying but Holy Communion does give me great spiritual strength.'

What clues do these two young Christians give as to the importance of Holy Communion for them?

What is the Mass?

When Roman Catholics celebrate Holy Communion they call it the Mass. For this service the priest wears special clothes to underline its importance. It is a service which always follows the same pattern.

The order of the Mass

The Mass is a drama. Each part of it underlines the sacrifice of Jesus on the cross. The worshipper is drawn more and more into the unfolding story.

- The priest begins by welcoming everyone to the service. He often uses familiar words to do this:

  'The grace of our Lord Jesus Christ, the love of God and the fellowship of the Holy Spirit be with you all.'

  Then everyone asks God's forgiveness for their sins. The priest may sprinkle the people with holy water to show that they have been forgiven.

- Next comes the Gloria Patri (see page 29), followed by readings from the Bible. Lay people may read from the Old Testament and the Epistles but the Gospel is always read by a priest or a deacon. A sermon follows.

- A well-known Creed, the Nicene, from the fourth century, is recited by everyone. This creed expresses what the Church believes about God the Father, Jesus Christ, the Holy Spirit and the Church (see pages 44-5).

  Five prayers are then said (the prayers of the faithful) for the needs of the Church, the world and the local community.

- The offertory takes place in which bread, wine and money are offered to God.

- The Eucharistic prayers, including a prayer of thanksgiving, are said. At the heart of these prayers is the consecration of the bread and wine. As the priest recites the words of Jesus at the Last Supper so the people believe that Christ becomes present in the bread and wine. The people then join in with three public statements (called acclamations):

  'Christ has died.
  Christ is risen.
  Christ will come again.'

Why does the priest wear special clothes for the Mass?

- The Our Father (the Lord's Prayer) in which the people ask for the food of eternal life is repeated. As they all share in the same bread so they offer one another the kiss of peace.

- The act of communion follows. The priest and the people then take the bread and wine.

- The blessing and the command to love one another end the service. Everyone is then sent out into the world to do God's work.

What does the Mass mean?

There are two main parts:

- The Mass provides an opportunity for each worshipper to participate in the actual death of Jesus. This belief, called **transubstantiation**, is very difficult to understand. To eat the bread and drink the wine is the most important act of religious worship for a Catholic.

- Sharing in the Mass must result in the worshipper going out to meet the needs of the poor. The two are very closely connected. Without feeling more responsible for the needs of his fellow human beings the Catholic has missed the deeper meaning of the Mass.

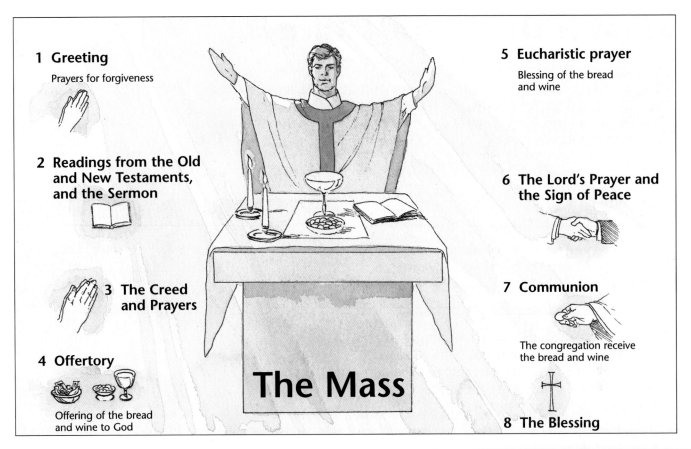

1 Greeting

Prayers for forgiveness

2 Readings from the Old and New Testaments, and the Sermon

3 The Creed and Prayers

4 Offertory

Offering of the bread and wine to God

The Mass

5 Eucharistic prayer

Blessing of the bread and wine

6 The Lord's Prayer and the Sign of Peace

7 Communion

The congregation receive the bread and wine

8 The Blessing

- What name do Roman Catholics give to the service of Holy Communion?
- What is the act of consecration?
- What are the two most important parts of the Mass?

For your dictionary

Catholics believe **transubstantiation** takes place during the Mass when the bread and wine become the actual body and blood of Christ.

The priest is consecrating the bread. What are the three acclamations that the people make?

1 Can you explain how the wine goblet and the plate of wafers (bread) play an important part in the Mass?

2 In the Preface of the Holy Eucharist, this explanation is given for the Mass:

'He is the true and eternal priest who establishes this unending sacrifice. He offered himself as a victim for our deliverance and taught us to make this offering in his memory. As we eat his body which he gave for us, we grow in strength. As we drink his blood which is poured out for us we are washed clean.'

a Who is the 'true and eternal priest' who has died for the sins of the world?

b What happens to each person as they eat the body (bread) of Jesus?

c What happens as the people drink the blood (wine) of Jesus?

What is the Divine Liturgy?

In the Orthodox Church, Holy Communion becomes the Divine Liturgy, or the 'work of the people'. Orthodox Christians believe that worship is a human activity which is offered to God. Over the centuries the Liturgy has become fixed and today it follows the same pattern first laid down by St John Chrysostom in the fourth century.

The Divine Liturgy

This is the order of the Liturgy.

- The bread and wine are prepared. The priest repeats short prayers and the people respond with the same words:

  Kyrie eleison (Lord, have mercy).

- A Psalm and the Little Litany are sung, with the people again responding with 'Kyrie eleison'. The Beatitudes are read (see Exercise 1) before the Gospel is carried above the heads of the people as they sing three times:

  'Holy God, holy and mighty, holy and immortal, have mercy on us.'

- The Grand Entrance, as servers process with candles and incense, follows whilst the priests carry the bread and the wine. The people bow as the procession passes and the Royal Doors are opened, allowing the priests to pass through into the sanctuary. The bread and wine are laid on the Holy Table – the altar.

- The people greet one another with the kiss of peace before reciting the Nicene Creed (see page 45). In the prayers which follow, the story of the Last Supper is retold before everyone joins in the Lord's Prayer. Finally, the priest raises the bread and breaks it. This part of the service is called the elevation. The choir then sings and bells are rung.

- The priest comes and stands in front of the Royal Doors and those receiving Communion come forward and kneel. They receive a piece of holy bread dipped in wine and served on a spoon.

- After taking Communion, everyone comes up to kiss the cross which the priest holds and a small piece of bread is shared together as a sign of fellowship and love, just like the meals that the early Christians used to share together.

What lies behind the Royal Doors? Why do you think that the bread and wine are offered there before they are given to the people?

Why is the Liturgy so important?

There are millions of Orthodox Christians throughout the world and the Divine Liturgy is very important to them. They know that if they attend any Orthodox church the service will be exactly the same. Through the Liturgy each believer is linked to their brothers and sisters, past and present, who have celebrated the same service. What's more, centuries of prayer and devotion have gone into making the service what it is today. As a result it is like a reservoir of beautiful words and pictures which the worshipper is free to use and draw upon.

- What is the Divine Liturgy in the Orthodox Church?
- What part of the Divine Liturgy is called the elevation?
- How do members of the congregation receive Communion?

In the Orthodox Church the bread and wine are served on a spoon. Why do you think Communion is given in this way?

1 The reading of the Beatitudes plays an important part in the Divine Liturgy. Read them in Matthew 5.3–10, then copy and complete this table in your exercise book.

Verse	'Blessed are the...'	'for they shall...'
3	poor in spirit	inherit the Kingdom of God.
———	———	be comforted.
———	———	inherit the earth.
———	———	be filled.
———	merciful	———
———	pure in heart	———
———	peacemakers	———

Why do you think that the Beatitudes are read during the Divine Liturgy?

2 Here are six words which are used in this chapter. The letters are all scrambled up. Unscramble them and then explain in your own words what they mean.

a RILUTYG
b YEKIR NEELISO
c TBSETUEDIA
d NINEEC DRECE
e ENVELOAIT
f ARYLO ODSOR

What is the Lord's Supper?

Of the Free Churches, the Quakers and the Salvation Army do not celebrate any of the sacraments, including Holy Communion. Although Methodists often use the term 'Holy Communion', Free Churches have two other favourite titles:

- The Breaking of Bread – a term taken from the New Testament (Acts 20.7).

- The Lord's Supper – an expression used by Paul (1 Corinthians 11.20).

The Lord's Supper

Although each Christian denomination has its own ideas about celebrating the Lord's Supper there are four common elements:

- The Bible and the sermon. After listening to the reading of a passage connected with the Lord's Supper, such as Luke 22.7–23 or 1 Corinthians 11.17–34, the minister explains the meaning of the service.

- The bread and wine are either placed on the Communion table – there is no altar in Free Churches – or a cloth covering them is removed. The bread and wine are then consecrated to God.

- The congregation remains seated whilst a loaf of bread is passed round. Each person breaks off a small piece before the loaf is passed on. They eat the bread at once without waiting for anyone else. This is important because Protestants believe that each person must respond to God for themselves.

  The wine is then delivered to them on slotted trays in tiny glasses by the leaders of the church. When everyone has received their glass the people drink together as a mark of their unity in Christ.

- A final thanksgiving and blessing end the service. The people are encouraged to go out into the world to serve God and spread the Christian Gospel.

The meaning of the Lord's Supper

Unlike Roman Catholics, Protestants do not believe that anything happens to the bread and wine during the service. They simply remain symbols which prompt the people into thinking more deeply about the death of Jesus. As they are consumed so the believer's mind and heart go back to the events which happened at Calvary. The minister has already encouraged them to do this by telling them to eat the bread and drink the wine whilst 'feeding on him (Christ) in your hearts by faith'.

What does the drinking of wine symbolise in the Lord's Supper?

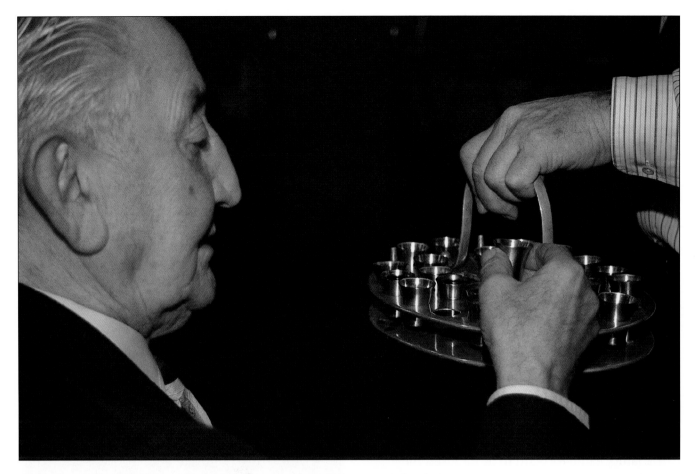

In most Free Churches the bread and wine are taken to the people by the leaders of the church. Why do you think they do this?

Paul claimed to have had a special revelation from God about the Lord's Supper (1 Corinthians 11.23–25). This is what he wrote:

'For I received from the Lord what I also passed on to you. The Lord Jesus, on the night he was betrayed, took bread, and when he had given thanks, he broke it and said, "This is my body, which is for you, do this in remembrance of me." In the same way, after supper he took the cup, saying, "This cup is the new covenant in my blood, do this, whenever you drink it, in remembrance of me."'

The answers to questions **a–e** can be found in this quotation:

a What did Paul receive from the Lord and what did he do with it?
b When did Jesus share his last meal with his disciples?
c What did Jesus do after he had broken the bread in front of his disciples?
d Why did Jesus tell his disciples that they should 'break bread' with one another?
e Why should the disciples drink wine together?
These questions are a little bit more difficult:
f Can you find out what the word 'covenant' means and then try to explain why it is used here?
g How do the Free Churches try to stick as closely as possible to these words of Paul?

- Which two names do Free Churches give to the service of Holy Communion and why?
- Who brings the bread and wine to the people during the Lord's Supper?
- What does the minister tell the people to do before they eat the bread and drink the wine?

What are the Creeds?

Can you say exactly what you think a Christian is? Could it be someone who goes to church regularly; someone who sets out to help their neighbour; someone who prays; someone who shows a high level of commitment to Christ and the Church or someone who believes certain things? The answer is probably to be found in a combination of all these things and a few more besides. No one, though, can dispute the importance of Christian belief.

The Creeds

In the past the Church has used its beliefs to draw a line between those who are acceptable to the Church and those who are not. People who hold unacceptable beliefs have been called **heretics** and thrown out of the Church. To be able to do this, the Church needed a clear statement of its own beliefs and this is where the Creeds have come in.

There was also another reason why a clear statement of belief was required. When young converts to Christianity came forward to be baptised they were expected to make an open statement of what they believed. Certain correct and acceptable formulae developed for them to use and it was from these formulae that the Creeds developed.

In the Church's history there have been two important creeds and both of them are very old:

- The Nicene Creed. An important Church Council met in Nicea in 325 under Emperor Constantine. The Creed that it produced was the most important in the Church's history.

- The Apostles Creed. People once thought that this Creed came from the original disciples of Jesus, but it didn't. It was produced early in the fifth century.

Using the Creeds

Although both Creeds are ancient, they are still used regularly in worship today by the Orthodox, Anglican and Catholic Churches. At some point, in most services, the people turn towards the altar and say the Creed together. Why? Religious belief, like everything else, has changed over the centuries and many Christians find it impossible to accept and believe all the statements in the Creeds.

The Creeds have a different use nowadays. When the members of a congregation recite the words together they are not trying to express what they believe as much as announcing that what unites them as Christians is greater than anything that divides them. The surprising thing is that there have been very few attempts over the centuries to update the Creeds.

Many Churches make no use of them at all in their worship. Some Churches have their own 'Statements of Faith' but these play no part in their worship. Others simply accept that the vast majority of people joining in their worship more or less believe the same things.

Belief is important to Christians. What do you think that Christians might learn about God from the way that a mother looks after her baby?

1 Here are two short extracts from the most important Creeds. Look at them carefully.

The Apostles Creed

'I believe in God the Father Almighty, creator of heaven and earth. I believe in Jesus Christ, his only Son, our Lord. He was conceived by the power of the Holy Spirit and born of the Virgin Mary. He suffered under Pontius Pilate, was crucified, died and was buried. On the third day he rose again...'

The Nicene Creed

'We believe in one God – We believe in one Lord, Jesus Christ – God from God, Light from Light, true God from true God – For us men and our salvation he came down from heaven; by the power of the Holy Spirit he became incarnate of the Virgin Mary and was made man. For our sake he was crucified under Pontius Pilate; he suffered death and was buried. On the third day he rose again...'

Draw up a table, like the one below, of the different things that these creeds say about different aspects of Christian belief.

Belief	Apostles Creed	Nicene Creed
God	1 2	1 2
Jesus The Holy Spirit The Church		

What do you know about the backgrounds to the Apostles and Nicene Creeds?

2 Here are two photographs. Which statements in the Creeds do they illustrate?

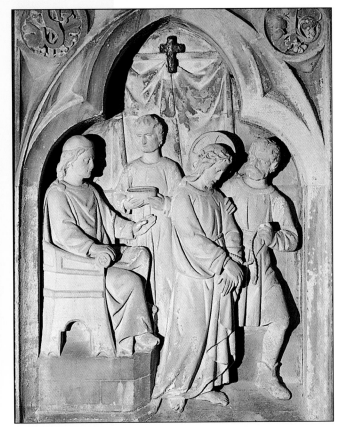

Draw your own illustrations for two more statements in the Creeds.

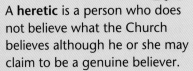

For your dictionary
A **heretic** is a person who does not believe what the Church believes although he or she may claim to be a genuine believer.

- What is a creed?
- Which two creeds has the Church used in its worship over the centuries?
- Why were creeds considered necessary in the first place?

How important is music in Christian worship?

What kind of music do you enjoy? Are your musical tastes similar or different from those of your parents and your friends? In the past, the Church has provided some of the best, and most popular, music. Some of the greatest composers, such as Bach, have written much church, or religious, music. This is because music has always played a very important part in Christian worship.

profile. As a result, cathedral choirs often reach a very high standard indeed. In many services the choir sing on behalf of the members of the congregation instead of singing to them. In this way the choir's contribution becomes a vital element in the worship. The same thing happens in many of the larger Orthodox churches.

Since the Middle Ages, most churches have had an organ. Although they were outlawed for a short time by the Puritans, the pipe organ established itself as being ideal for leading the worship and the music in the larger church buildings. Sometimes the organist plays pieces of music at the start and the end of the service for the people to listen to. These are called 'voluntaries'.

Do you think this is a way to bring people back into church, especially young people?

Choirs and the organ

Choirs have been a part of Church worship since the fourth century. In many churches a choir still leads the singing. In most churches the members of the choir are drawn from the congregation but some cathedrals have professional choristers, often including boys taken from their own cathedral school. As you can imagine, the curriculum of a cathedral school is rather different from the normal one, with music and singing having a much higher

Why do you think that many smaller churches now use a piano or a group of musicians or singers to lead the worship?

Hymns

Pieces of music written especially to be sung in a church are called **hymns**. The tradition of hymn-singing is strongest in the Free Churches, many of which were born during a time of 'religious revival' when music played a very important part. Hymn-singing plays a particularly important part in the worship of two denominations:

- the Methodists. Perhaps the greatest hymn writer of all time was Charles Wesley, the brother of John, whose teaching led to the formation of the Methodist Church. Many people would say that the *Methodist Hymn Book* was the greatest collection of hymns ever put together. Whilst Wesley's hymns are most precious to Methodists, they are used by Christians from all denominations.

- the Salvation Army. General Booth, the founder of the Salvation Army asked the famous question:

'Why should the Devil have all the best tunes?'

He then proceeded to write many hymns which the bands of the Army accompanied in rousing fashion.

In contrast, all singing in the Orthodox Church is unaccompanied, as was the music of the early Christians. Quakers do not include any music in their service.

---

1 In this crossword the answers have been supplied but the clues are missing. Make up your own clues to go with the answers.

For your dictionary

A **hymn** is a collection of words, or poetry, set to music for a Christian congregation to sing.

- What are pieces of music written especially to be sung in church called?
- What are pieces of music called which are played at the beginning and end of church services?
- Which Church sings its music unaccompanied and which denomination has no music at all in its services?

2 Copy out these sentences and fill in the blanks from the choices below.

a _____ was a famous composer of Christian music.
b _____ , which date from the fourth century, often lead the singing in churches today.
c Many hymns sung by _____ were written by _____ _____ .
d _____ _____ , the founder of the _____ _____ , once wondered why the Devil should have all the best tunes.

**Choirs   Methodists   Salvation Army   Bach
Charles Wesley   William Booth**

What are Christian communities?

Whilst most Christians live pretty ordinary lives, perhaps pursuing a career, getting married, bringing up a family and trying to make ends meet etc., a few leave their family and friends behind to join a religious community. There are many reasons why someone should want to do this but most feel that they have some kind of **vocation** – a calling from God to do so.

A religious community

The first Christian communities were formed about 1600 years ago in Egypt. Some of them grew to be so large that they had thousands of members. From the beginning these communities were single-sex. A community of monks live in a **monastery**, whilst a group of nuns occupy a **convent**. Each community expects its members to take a traditional three-fold vow:

- the vow of poverty. A monk or a nun is expected to give up all their possessions before entering the religious order. From the moment that they enter the order they possess nothing of their own.

- the vow of obedience. Each person must be prepared to obey the rules of the religious community and God. A solicitor or a university professor who joins a community may find themselves digging the garden today and scrubbing the floor tomorrow – all to learn

Here you can see a novice nun (on the left) who has not yet taken her vows dressed differently from the fully professed nun on the right. Why do you think that she has to do this?

obedience. Why do you think that this is a particularly important lesson to learn if one is going to live in a religious community?

- the vow of chastity. This means not having a physical, sexual relationship with another person. It means not loving anything or anyone more than God. Monks and nuns do not marry although some people leave their religious order to do so.

Which of these three vows do you think most people would find the most difficult to keep?

Living in a religious community

In the Western world it was St Benedict who laid down the rules by which most convents and monasteries have been run, called 'The Rule of St Benedict'. Insisting that all monks should pray and work hard St Benedict laid down seven times of prayer and worship for each day (see opposite).

There are many religious communities. Amongst the most well-known are the **Franciscans**, who took their name from St Francis of Assisi in the thirteenth century. This saint had a great reputation for being able to make friends with all forms of life. The birds listened attentively to all his best sermons before he preached them to the people! The Franciscans were soon followed by the Poor Clares, an order of nuns. St Clare lived at the same time as Francis and, like him, she lived a life of prayer and poverty. The **Jesuits**, a teaching order of monks founded in the sixteenth century by St Ignatius of Loyola, demand the traditional three vows from all monks plus a fourth: total obedience to the Pope, the Bishop of Rome.

The Taizé community in France, known worldwide for its haunting music and chants, has members from several different Christian denominations although all of its members are monks. Thousands visit the community every year to share in its worship and life. The Iona community, in Scotland, is not made up of monks or nuns. To be a member of the community people have to commit themselves to pray and work for peace in their own community, to support the community financially and to spend a week each year on the island. Many people believe that Taizé and Iona offer the way forward for religious communities into the twenty-first century.

Find out all that you can about either the Taizé (left) or the Iona communities (right).

1 Imagine that you are a Roman Catholic or an Anglican who has decided to enter a convent or a monastery. Write to one of the following:

a   your grandmother *or*
b   your parents *or*
c   your boyfriend or girlfriend.

Try to explain your decision and ask for their support and understanding in the future. You might even be brave enough to try to write the reply that you think they might send!

2 This is the daily timetable followed by Benedictine and other monks.

LAUDS	3.00 a.m.
PRIME	6.00 a.m.
TERCE	9.00 a.m.
SEXT	Noon
NONE	3.00 p.m.
VESPERS	Evening Prayer
COMPLINE	Final Night Prayer

a   Who first laid down the timetable followed by Benedictine monks?
b   What is the first service of the day?
c   Can you find out why the last service of the day is called 'Compline'? Clue: It is to do with the meaning of the word.
d   If you were a Benedictine monk what would you find most difficult about your daily timetable?

For your dictionary

A **convent** is the home of nuns.
The **Franciscans** are a Christian order of monks founded by St Francis of Assisi.
A **Jesuit** is a member of the Society of Jesus, formed by St Ignatius of Loyola.
A **monastery** is the home of monks.
A person is said to have a **vocation** if they feel called by God to follow a certain way of life.

- What is a vocation?
- What are the three vows taken by those entering a religious community?
- Why is St Benedict important?

Christians and celebration
What are Advent and Christmas?

Most churches follow an unofficial 'Christian year'. It begins on the fourth Sunday before Christmas (either the last Sunday in November or the first in December). The season which runs between this Sunday and Christmas Day (25th December) is called **Advent**, a word which means 'coming'. The season makes Christians look both backwards to the birth of Jesus and forwards to the time when Jesus returns to the earth, as he promised to do.

Describe the scene shown in this South American crib.

Celebrating Advent

In many churches, people start to sing carols at the beginning of Advent. The readings from the Bible, the hymns and other symbols visible in church during Advent all underline the distinctive character of this time of the year.

In many churches people arrive for the Advent carol service to find the building in total darkness. As they enter, each person is handed a lighted candle and so the church is gradually bathed in light. What do you think that each member of the congregation is expected to understand by this?

Most of the Bible readings during the four Sundays of Advent come from the Old Testament, from the prophets who looked forward most keenly to the

coming of God's Messiah. Towards the end of Advent, readings about John the Baptist, God's messenger who prepared the way for Jesus, are introduced.

In some churches there is an Advent Crown, with four, or sometimes five, candles. One candle is lit on each Sunday in Advent to symbolise the light that is coming into the world through Jesus.

Christmas

At midnight on Christmas Eve, 24th December, church bells ring out across the world. Many Christians gather in church for Midnight Mass to thank God for his greatest gift to the human race: Jesus. Churches everywhere are specially decorated. A crib is often set up to show the traditional stable scene with the baby Jesus surrounded by Mary, Joseph and the animals.

Long before Christianity existed, 25th December was a special day. The shortest day of the year (21st December) was over and the people began to look forward to the return of the Unconquered Sun. On 25th December they celebrated its inevitable return. In the Roman Empire the festival that was held at this time was called 'Saturnalia'. In Europe it was called 'Yuletide', when evergreens were brought into the home to keep the spirit of life alive.

What do you think this is? What do the candles symbolise?

- What do Christians remember during Advent?
- How did Christians come to celebrate the birth of Jesus on 25th December?
- What is Epiphany?

For a long time, the Christians did not celebrate the birth of Jesus. They did not know when he had been born. It was only in the fourth century that they took over the Roman festival celebrating the birth of Mithras (the Unconquerable Sun) and turned it into a celebration of the birth of Jesus.

Epiphany

Originally, Epiphany (6th January) was the celebration of the baptism of Jesus. However, it soon came to commemorate the showing of Jesus to the first non-Jews (Gentiles), the Wise Men, in the Gospel story.

> ### For your dictionary
> **Advent** is the season in the Church during which Christians prepare themselves for the coming of Christ into the world.

1 Read the extract below of Isaiah 11.1–6, one of the most familiar Advent readings. Remember, as you read, that it is intended to prepare listeners for the coming of their Saviour, Jesus Christ.

Then a branch will grow from the stock of Jesse,
and a shoot will spring from its roots.
On him the Spirit of the Lord will rest:
a spirit of wisdom and understanding,
a spirit of counsel and power,
a spirit of knowledge and fear of the Lord;
and in the fear of the Lord will be his delight.
He will not judge by outward appearances
or decide a case on hearsay;
but with justice he will judge the poor…
Then the wolf will live with the lamb,
and the leopard will lie down with the kid;
the calf and the young lion will feed together,
with a little child to tend them.

a Isaiah is speaking here of a king yet to come. Who was this king's ancestor?
b What will this new king be given to help him rule over his people?
c How will the king rule over his people?
d How will the animals react to the rule of the new king?
e Why do you think that this passage is chosen to be read during Advent?

2 There is a passage in Isaiah that Christians have always taken to refer to John the Baptist:

A voice cries:
Clear a road through the wilderness for the Lord,
prepare a highway across the desert for our God.
(Isaiah 40.3)

Also during Advent, a Collect is read out:

Almighty God;
who sent your servant John the Baptist
to prepare your people for the coming of your Son…

a Why do you think that John the Baptist is often called the forerunner of Jesus?
b What did John the Baptist tell the people to do?
c Why do you think that John the Baptist is remembered during Advent?

What happens during Lent?

Easter is such an important Christian festival that there are 40 days of preparation leading up to it! These days of preparation are known as Lent. They start with Ash Wednesday and end with Holy Week which runs from Palm Sunday to Easter Sunday.

The temptation of Jesus

The story in the life of Jesus which is associated with Lent is that of Jesus going into the wilderness to be tempted by the Devil. Refresh your memory by reading Mark 1.12,13 and Luke 4.1–13. From these accounts you will be able to see why Lent is a time of **fasting** and penitence for many Christians.

Why keep Lent?

It's a very old custom dating back to the time in the early Christian Church when new converts to the faith were baptised at Easter. Before the Church was willing to baptise them, each person was expected to fast, which meant only eating one meal a day without any luxuries like meat and fish, for 40 days. That was the length of time that Jesus spent in the wilderness. The practice soon caught on and before long the whole Church was fasting in the weeks leading up to Easter. Why do you think that many Christians, over the centuries, have thought that fasting was good for their souls?

Few Christians today fast in quite the same way. Many do try to give up something for Lent and give the money that they save to charity. It may not be the same thing but at least other people benefit from their self-denial. Many churches run special prayer and study groups during Lent. It is a time when many Christians try to find out more about their own faith. In church, meanwhile, the dominant colour is purple, but can you work out why?

What is Shrove Tuesday?

The day before Lent begins is **Shrove Tuesday**. Better known as 'pancake day', Shrove Tuesday was the day on which people made pancakes to use up all the rich food in the house before Lent began. They also went to church to be 'shriven' (forgiven), hence the name Shrove Tuesday.

What happens on Ash Wednesday?

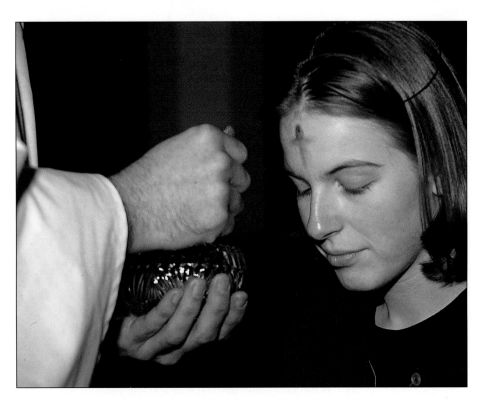

So Lent begins. On Ash Wednesday the priest in some churches makes the sign of the cross on the foreheads of worshippers at a special service. This is a sign of penitence, which means being sorry for one's sins. The ash has come from the burning of the previous year's palm crosses.

There is another reason for the ash marking. It reminds the worshipper that he or she is only as ashes in the sight of God. That is why the priest tells each of them, as he makes the sign of the cross:

'Remember, O man, that dust thou art and to dust thou shalt return.'

Why do you think that the worshipper is reminded of this at the beginning of Lent?

Why does a priest make an ash sign on the worshipper's forehead at the start of Lent?

This is the famous pancake race at Olney in Bucks. What is the link between pancakes and Shrove Tuesday?

- What is Lent?
- Why is Shrove Tuesday so called?
- What is the significance of Mothering Sunday?

When is Mothering Sunday?

Mothering Sunday is always on the fourth Sunday of Lent. It is the day on which people used to thank God for 'Mother' Church and the way it looks after or 'mothers' them. This is not the same as Mother's Day, which is a more recent invention, although the two have become combined.

After this, another week now passes before Holy Week begins with Palm Sunday.

For your dictionary 📖

Fasting means going without food, usually for religious reasons.
On **Mothering Sunday** people always thanked God for 'Mother' Church.
Shrove Tuesday is the last day before Lent begins and a time of preparation for the forthcoming fast.

1 Copy this chart into your exercise book. Make a drawing and write three sentences about each of these occasions to show that you understand what is special about them.

Shrove Tuesday
1
2
3

Ash Wednesday
1
2
3

Mothering Sunday
1
2
3

2 Copy the following sentences into your book. Complete each of them from the words or phrases listed below:

a The _____ days leading up to the celebration of _____ are called _____ .
b Before new _____ to Christianity could be _____ , they were expected to _____ for forty days.
c _____ _____ was so called because people used to go to church to be _____ or forgiven.
d On _____ _____ , worshippers have the _____ of the _____ placed on their foreheads as a sign that they are sorry for their sins.

Lent   fast   Shrove Tuesday   sign   forty

converts   Ash Wednesday   cross   Easter

baptised   shriven

What is Holy Week?

Everyone has serious as well as light moments. Christians are no exceptions. The most solemn time of the year for them begins with Holy Week when their thoughts turn to the last week in the life of Jesus. From the Gospels we learn that Jesus spent all of this time in or around the city of Jerusalem. Although the Gospels devote about 40 per cent of their space to these last few days, we cannot be sure that all of the events definitely took place during this week. One thing is very clear; the week that ended in tragedy actually began very differently.

Palm Sunday

Jews travelled to Jerusalem from all over the Roman Empire for their most important festival: Passover or Pesach. At this annual event, their minds went back to the time, hundreds of years earlier, when their ancestors escaped from slavery in Egypt. As a Jew, it was natural for Jesus to join the pilgrims as they made their way to Jerusalem.

Jesus arrived in the city on the back of a donkey. It caused quite a stir but why was he riding a donkey? Matthew in his Gospel tells us that Jesus was fulfilling prophecies from the Old Testament when he entered the city.

How do Christians today remember the first Palm Sunday? In many churches they are given a small palm cross to keep until the next Ash Wednesday. Can you remember what happens to the crosses then? Sometimes Christians take part in a procession which is led by a donkey.

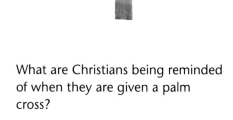

What are Christians being reminded of when they are given a palm cross?

Maundy Thursday

On the first Maundy Thursday, Jesus ate his last meal with his disciples. This was no ordinary meal. It was at this meal that Jesus astonished everyone by taking a towel and water to wash the feet of his disciples. It was astonishing because it was a task normally carried out by the lowest servant in the household. What do you think that Jesus was trying to teach his disciples by acting out this parable in front of them? The clue lies in the words that he told them:

'As I have loved you so you must love one another.' (John 13.34)

Jesus called this a new commandment. The Latin word for commandment is *mandatum*. Now you know why we call this day Maundy Thursday.

How is Maundy Thursday celebrated today? In the past, bishops, priests, popes and kings have washed the feet of their subjects on this day. The Queen gives out special coins, Maundy money, to elderly people. Can you find out how many coins each person receives?

The end of Holy Week

Holy Week ends in church with the most serious day in the whole Christian year: Good Friday. This is the day on which Christians remember the arrest, trial and crucifixion of Jesus.

- What is Holy Week and how does it begin?
- Which event is celebrated on Palm Sunday?
- What is Maundy Thursday?

1 a Why are the people in the photograph taking part in a procession led by a donkey?

b Imagine that you are living in a block of flats overlooking the road along which this procession is passing. Write a letter to a friend describing what you see and what you think is the significance of the procession.

2 Read Matthew 21.1–11. One Sunday, a large group of people gathered on the outskirts of Jerusalem. Meanwhile, in a village nearby, Jesus was speaking to two of his disciples.

What did he say to them?

When Jesus entered the city of Jerusalem the people were astonished. Why?

What did the people do when they saw Jesus?
How does Matthew describe the effect of this event on the city of Jerusalem?

3 When he entered Jerusalem on a donkey Jesus fulfilled two prophecies from the Old Testament. One of them is found in Zechariah 9.9 and the other in Psalm 118.26–7.

a Look up these two prophecies in a Bible and copy them into your exercise book.
b Describe two ways in which Jesus was believed to have fulfilled these words when he entered Jerusalem.

What is Good Friday?

The most important time of the year for all Christians is Easter, so much so that Christianity has been called an 'Easter Faith'. The most important elements of Christian belief have their basis in the events of Good Friday and Easter Sunday. On Good Friday Christians remember the death of Jesus whilst on Easter Sunday they commemorate his resurrection from the dead.

What is being remembered?

According to the Gospels Jesus was put to death by the Romans on a cross, a very cruel form of execution known as **crucifixion**. His crime was to claim to be the King of the Jews. This claim frightened both the Jewish and the Roman leaders but can you work out why?

It seems strange to call the day on which Jesus was put to death *Good* Friday. What could possibly be good about it? The answer is that the day has always been known as Good Friday because of the goodness of Jesus. Christians believe that in dying on the cross for the sins of the world Jesus was showing God's love to everyone.

How is Good Friday celebrated?

Good Friday is a day of deep sadness in the Christian community. In many churches the whole building is stripped bare – there are no flowers or candles, no colour, and crucifixes and crosses are covered or hidden from sight. Everything is designed to remind the worshipper that, after eating a last meal with his closest friends, Jesus suffered a lonely and agonising death.

Some Christians try to enter into that loneliness. They spend the hours between 12.00 noon and 3.00 p.m. (the time when Jesus was on the cross) meditating on the last words of Jesus. In some places, Christians march through their local town on Good Friday, led by someone carrying a wooden cross.

In Orthodox churches Christians hold a kind of funeral for Jesus on Good Friday. A cloth bearing an image of the dead Christ is carried into the centre of the church. The worshippers then follow the cloth in procession around the outside of the building as church bells ring. Finally the cloth is brought back into the middle of the church to remind worshippers of the burial of Christ in a stone tomb. Why do you think that it is important for some Christians to dramatise the death of Christ?

Why do we eat hot-cross buns?

Hot-cross buns are traditionally eaten on Good Friday. The cross on top of the bun, of course, symbolises the cross of Jesus. The spices in the bun are a reminder of those spices which Jews traditionally wrapped around bodies before burial. They were eaten by worshippers breaking the fast of Lent and so these symbols were extremely powerful.

What was crucifixion?

Why do you think these Christians are following a cross on Good Friday?

- Which is the most important Christian festival?
- What is remembered by all Christians on Good Friday?
- How do Orthodox Christians commemorate the death of Jesus?

For your dictionary

Crucifixion A form of execution used by the Romans, by which the criminal was nailed to a cross of wood until they died.

Why is this particular symbol associated with Good Friday?

1 'It seems very strange that Jesus was put to death on Good Friday and yet we call the day 'Good'. Why?'

'Because Christians believe that God brought so much good out of what could have been a tragic event. They believe, for instance, that people can have their sins forgiven because Jesus died for them. That is why it is called Good Friday'.

What do you think of that?

2 According to the Gospels, Jesus said seven things from the cross. Copy this table into your exercise book, look up each of the references and fill in the spaces.

Reference	The words of Jesus	Spoken to whom?
Luke 23.34		
Luke 23.43		
John 19.26		
Mark 15.34		
John 19.28		
John 19.30		
Luke 23.46		

What is Easter Sunday?

Do you know which is the most important day in the whole Christian year? Christmas Day? Good Friday? No. The answer is Easter Sunday. This is the day on which Christians throughout the world celebrate the rising of Jesus from the dead: the Resurrection. Paul believed that if Jesus had not risen from the dead the Christian faith would have been meaningless.

How is Easter celebrated?

The word 'Easter' has ancient origins. It is probably named after the Anglo-Saxon goddess of Spring, Eostre. Ever since Christians adopted the festival, the date has been fixed each year by the position of the moon. In practice, Easter can fall any time between 21 March and April 24.

The first celebration of Easter usually occurs on the Saturday evening or before dawn on the Sunday morning. This is because the women who found the tomb of Jesus empty went there before sunrise. It seems, therefore, that Jesus must have risen from the dead sometime during Saturday night. In many Anglican, Catholic and Orthodox churches Easter services start late on the Saturday night. The service itself is called a vigil. Can you suggest why? What do the people imagine that they are doing? The vigil begins with the church in total darkness although one or two candles illuminate a Bible from which a series of extracts are read. Everyone is holding a candle although none of them are yet alight.

After the readings the priest lights a fire at the back of the church and from this lights the **Paschal** candle. The light is then taken to the front of the church in a procession stopping three times as the priest says: *'The light of Christ'*, to which the people reply, *'Thanks be to God.'*

Each time this happens, a few candles are lit and they pass the light on to other candles. From the front of the church the light gradually spreads as the doors are swung open and the priest announces in a loud voice: *'The Lord is risen'*, and the people reply, *'He is risen indeed.'*

The people turn to one another and greet each other with a holy kiss. Church bells are rung for the first time in three days and the people share a Eucharist meal. Together they have all just shared in one of the oldest of all Christian services: the Easter Vigil.

Easter traditions

There are many traditions associated with Easter Sunday. Easter gardens are models of a tomb in a real garden of flowers and herbs with three empty crosses standing above. Easter eggs symbolise the new life associated with the resurrection of Jesus. The open egg is a reminder of the empty tomb. Orthodox Christians often crack hardboiled eggs against each other saying 'Christ is risen'. All of which underlines the Christian belief that Easter is not just a time to remember; it is a time to experience and enjoy.

For your dictionary
The word **Paschal** comes from the word for Passover and describes anything related to Easter.

- What do Christians celebrate on Easter Sunday?
- What is the Easter Vigil?
- Which traditions underline the belief that Easter is a time for new life?

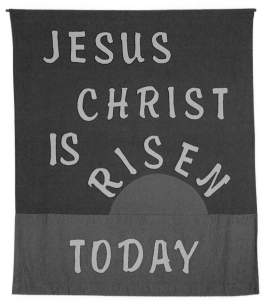

How would you sum up the meaning of Easter Day for a Christian believer?

There have been many paintings of the resurrection of Christ. Each of them tries to capture something special about the event. What do you think this painting by Stanley Spencer is trying to say?

1 In one of his letters, Paul underlined the importance of the Resurrection of Jesus to all Christians. He wrote:

'If Christ had not been raised, your faith is futile, and you are still in your sins.' (1 Corinthians 15.17)

Read Mark 16.1–6

a Who came to anoint the body of Jesus?

b What did they find?

c What did they see inside the tomb?

d What were they told?

2 *'For me, Easter is the most important time of the year. It is the time when Jesus died and rose again from the dead.'*

'I love the drama and excitement associated with the celebration of Easter. It is a time when the Church seems to come alive.'

'Although other people may find Easter a lively and colourful time, for me it is mostly a time for quiet reflection. When you think about it, everything depends upon life following death.'

Look at these three quotations carefully. Do you agree with any, or all, of them? Make up a quotation to express your own feelings about Easter or Spring.

What are Ascension Day and Whitsun?

Whilst they do not rank amongst the most important Christian festivals, Ascension Day and Whitsun are still widely celebrated. After this, several months pass before the whole cycle begins again with Advent.

What is Ascension Day?

Forty days after Easter, Christians celebrate the ascension of Jesus when, according to Luke's Gospel and the Acts of the Apostles, he left the earth and 'went up' into heaven. Before he did so, however, he told his disciples that God's Holy Spirit would inspire them to tell everyone about him. Luke's description then continues:

'After he said this, he was taken up before their very eyes, and a cloud hid him from their sight.' (Acts 1.8)

In the Bible, clouds are often said to hide God from human sight. Why do you think this is?

Ascension Day always falls on a Thursday but it is only a public holiday in a few countries. Many Christians ignore the day altogether and there are no widespread customs associated with it in this country. In the Anglican and Orthodox churches where it is celebrated, however, there is usually a special Eucharist.

Ten days later, on the seventh Sunday after Easter, comes Pentecost or Whit Sunday.

What is Pentecost?

Pentecost is a Jewish festival which has been taken over, and given another meaning, by the Christian Church. The word 'Pentecost' comes from the Greek word meaning 'fifty days'. That is why it is celebrated on the seventh Sunday, 50 days after Easter. On this day Christians celebrate the giving of the Holy Spirit to the first Christians on the day of Pentecost. You can read Luke's description of what happened to the disciples in Acts 2.1–12.

Pentecost became known as the birthday of the Christian Church and it is not difficult to see why. It became a popular time of the year to hold baptisms. In this country people who were baptised and confirmed at Pentecost wore white clothes and Pentecost became known as 'White Sunday' or Whit Sunday. Why do you think that people wore white clothes when they were baptised?

Inside many churches the dominant colour for this festival is red because of the flames of fire above the heads of the disciples on the Day of Pentecost.

If you look at Mark 1.1–11 you can discover why the Holy Spirit is traditionally associated with baptism – appearing in the form of a dove at the baptism of Jesus. Ever since the story of Noah's Ark (Genesis 8.8), the main symbol of the Holy Spirit has been a dove, the symbol of peace.

Design your own banner or stained-glass window to depict either the Ascension of Christ or the giving of the Holy Spirit at Pentecost.

This banner comes from the Roman Catholic Cathedral in Liverpool. It represents the Pope visiting Liverpool and links that visit with the giving of the Holy Spirit at Pentecost. Why do you think it makes this link?

- Which event in the life of Jesus is celebrated on Ascension Day?
- What does Pentecost mean?
- What do Christians celebrate at Whitsun and why is this festival so called?

1 In the New Testament, there are two descriptions of the ascension of Jesus into heaven, both written by Luke. Read Luke 24.50–3 and Acts 1.6–9 and then write down four pieces of information about the ascension of Jesus that we learn from each account.

Answer these questions:

a Where did the ascension of Jesus take place?

b What promise did Jesus give to his disciples before he left them?

c Where were the disciples to be witnesses and who would give them the necessary power?

d What did the disciples do after Jesus left them?

2 Imagine that you are living in an earlier period of time and that you have been baptised into the Christian Church at Whitsun. Write an entry for your journal describing the occasion, your clothes, what happened etc.

The actual procedure for baptism has hardly varied at all. You may decide to set your baptism in a period with which you are familiar. Otherwise you might need to do some research to make it authentic.

What is infant baptism?

Has a baby been born in your family recently? If so, you will have experienced at first hand the excitement that a new baby brings. Everyone may have been rather nervous until the baby is born. Now the celebrations can begin. Part of those celebrations, for many parents, is to bring the child to church to be baptised. This usually takes place a few weeks after the baby has been born, although Roman Catholics like to baptise babies as early as possible.

What is infant baptism?

To Christians, belonging to Church is like belonging to a family – God's family. When a new baby is born, they want him or her to be welcomed into that family. In a Baptist Church new parents bring their baby to be dedicated to God. Roman Catholic, Orthodox and Anglican churches, baptise babies. This service is sometimes called a Christening.

Before the service takes place the child's parents choose **godparents**. This is an old tradition. The various services make it clear that the godparents are expected to look after the child's spiritual welfare in the years ahead. Were you baptised? If so, do you know who your godparents are? Have they taken an interest in your spiritual welfare?

The baptismal service

In an Anglican church baptism the parents, godparents and the baby gather with the vicar around the **font**. The priest asks the parents and godparents a series of questions (see opposite). He then uses the water to make the sign of the cross on the baby's forehead before tipping water over its head three times. (This is usually the point at which the baby begins to cry!) Why do this three times? The answer lies in the words that the priest says as he or she does so:

'I baptise you in the name of the Father, and of the Son and of the Holy Spirit.'

As you might imagine, the different Churches have their own distinctive way of doing things. In some Methodist churches, for example, the parents are handed a lighted candle as the child is told:

'I give you this sign, for now you belong to Christ, the light of the world. Let your light shine before men that they might see your good works and give glory to your Father who is in heaven.'

The same thing can happen in an Anglican church. Why do you think they say these words to the baby when he or she doesn't understand what is happening?

What does infant baptism mean?

There are many couples who bring their babies to be baptised who do not understand or believe in what is going on. They come simply because it is a tradition. Others, though, find three main reasons behind the ceremony:

- The service is their way of thanking God for the safe delivery of their baby. In the past, this was more important than it is today because a mother often died giving birth.

- For many people, baptism is the ceremony through which a baby becomes a member of God's family – the Church.

- The water with which the baby is baptised is a sign – of cleansing from sin.

Why do you think that the baptismal font is located just inside the door of most traditional Anglican and Catholic churches?

What does the water used in baptism signify?

- Why are babies baptised?
- What part are the godparents expected to play in the life of a baby who has been baptised?
- Why are parents handed a lighted candle during some baptismal ceremonies?

During a service of infant baptism the vicar asks both parents and godparents two sets of questions:

1   *'Do you turn to Christ?'*
'I turn to Christ.'
'Do you repent of your sins?'
'I repent of my sins.'
'Do you renounce evil?'
'I renounce evil.'

2   *'Do you believe and trust in God?'*
'I believe and trust in him.'
'Do you believe and trust in Jesus Christ who
    redeemed the world?'
'I believe and trust in him.'
'Do you believe and trust in his Holy Spirit, who
    gives life to the people of God.'
'I believe and trust in him.'

a   In which Christian Churches is a scene like this likely to be taking place?
b   Who answers each of the questions?
c   Why does the vicar pour water over the baby's head?
d   Why do you think that this ceremony is carried out in public and not in private?
e   Can you find out what difference there is between Anglicans and Catholics on the one hand and Orthodox believers on the other in the way that they baptise babies?
f   Do you think that any baby should be baptised whether or not its parents go to church?
g   What do you think is the value of infant baptism? Will you have your own children baptised?

What is confirmation?

During infant baptism the baby does not understand what is happening. That is why another service is needed when the baby has grown up and is able to give his or her own agreement to the baptismal promises. That service is called Confirmation.

When is confirmation performed?

Confirmation is held only in those Churches which practise infant baptism. There is no standard age at which it is performed and the person involved can be any age from a teenager onwards. What matters is that each person is able to make their own commitment to the Christian way of life. To do this they make again (confirm) the promises that their parents and godparents made for them when they were baptised.

The Confirmation Service

In the Anglican and Catholic Churches, confirmation is performed only by a **bishop**. He asks each person about their religious faith and then places his hands upon their heads – called 'the laying on of hands'. This is a very old custom dating back to the New Testament. Traditionally it has been believed to be the means by which the Holy Spirit is given to the person.

In Roman Catholic confirmation services two other things take place:

- The bishop makes the sign of the cross on each person's forehead with oil. This is a sign of inner healing. Can you think why?

- The bishop slaps the face of each person lightly with two fingers. This is a sign that all of the sins that the person has committed since they were baptised have been forgiven. This is strange thing for a bishop to do but can you think of any possible explanation?

Why is confirmation important?

In the Orthodox Church baptism and confirmation are combined in a single service. Many Free Churches do not have an equivalent service to confirmation.

Yet, for Anglicans and Catholics, the service does have a considerable importance. After people have been confirmed they are accepted as full members of the Church and so are allowed to take the sacrament which represents the body and blood of Christ. Can you remember what this sacrament is called in the Anglican Church and in the Roman Catholic Church? Most Christians find that taking this sacrament gives them strength to live the Christian life day by day.

You can tell that the priest leading this procession is a bishop because he is carrying a crook. Find out why a bishop carries a shepherd's crook.

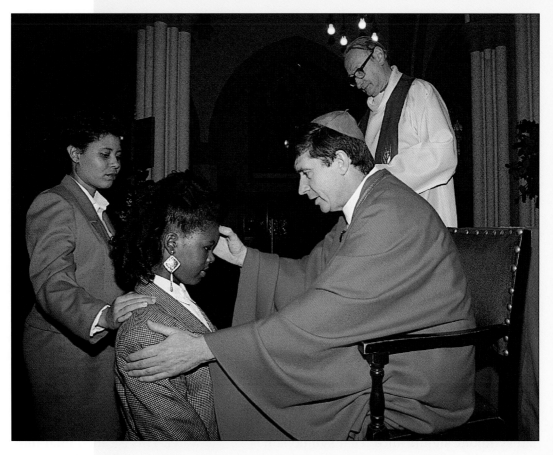

• What is the relationship between infant baptism and confirmation?
• Why does the bishop lay his hands upon the head of each person being confirmed?
• What is likely to be the main importance of confirmation in the lives of many Christians?

 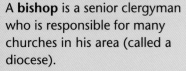
1 a Who carries out the Confirmation Service in an Anglican church?
    b What is the purpose of confirmation?
    c What do some Christians believe happens in a Confirmation Service?

2 Confirmation is a ceremony of commitment. Different Christian Churches have their own services of commitment. Find out about some of them and enter your findings on a table like the one below:

Church	Ceremony	Characteristics
Anglican	1	
	2	
	3	
Roman Catholic	1	
	2	
	3	
Methodist	1	
	2	
	3	
Orthodox	1	
	2	
	3	
Baptist	1	
	2	
	3	

What is adult baptism?

The Baptist Church is not the only Church which strongly believes in baptism as the Anglican, Catholic and Orthodox Churches also baptise. There is one important difference, though. The Baptist Church only baptises adults. They call this believer's baptism.

What is believer's baptism?

The Baptists cannot see how a young baby can have faith and no one should be baptised without such faith. This is why Baptists argue that it is much better to wait for baptism until a person becomes an adult and are able to make up their own mind about God. Do you agree? If so, at what age do you think a person is really old enough to decide whether they have faith in Jesus Christ or not?

In the past the clothes that people wore for baptism had symbolic significance. That symbolism is continued today when men wear a white shirt and grey trousers and women wear white dresses. White is a symbol of purity and baptism is a ceremony of cleansing.

Whilst a baptism is usually carried out in a pool sunk into the floor of the church it can be performed in a local river or the sea. Some pilgrims even travel to the Holy Land to be baptised in the River Jordan, just as Jesus was.

The service in a church begins with the person being baptised telling the congregation how they came to believe in Jesus Christ. This is called 'giving a testimony' and forms an essential part of most adult baptismal services. He or she then walks down a few steps at one end of the pool to join the Church minister in the water. After announcing that the person is being baptised because of their faith in Jesus Christ the minister rocks them gently backwards until their whole body is beneath the water. This is called **total immersion**.

- Which Church believes most strongly in the baptism of adults?
- What is meant by total immersion?
- What is the significance of adult baptism?

For your dictionary

Baptism by **total immersion** means that the person being baptised is completely submerged beneath the water.

These adults are being baptised in the River Jordan by total immersion. What do you think is the significance of being baptised in this particular river? See Mark 3.1–11.

Water is one of the most powerful Christian symbols. It indicates that a person has been washed and cleansed of their sins. What is the specific symbolism behind adult baptism?

- As the person goes down into the water it demonstrates that they are leaving their old, sinful life behind.

- As the person is beneath the water they are being 'buried' with Christ and so are dead with him.

- As the person leaves the pool so they enter the new life which God is now offering them.

As you can see, Baptists draw a strong parallel between adult baptism and the death, burial and resurrection of Jesus. Nothing takes place during the actual ceremony. No one is saved or forgiven because they have been baptised. It is of symbolic importance alone. What matters is that the person being baptised has demonstrated in public his or her own faith in Jesus Christ and shown a willingness to follow in his footsteps.

1 Adult believer's baptism is a highly symbolic act. Here you can see three drawings: before, during and after such a baptism. Draw your own pictures in your exercise book and explain in two sentences under each of them the symbolism behind the act.

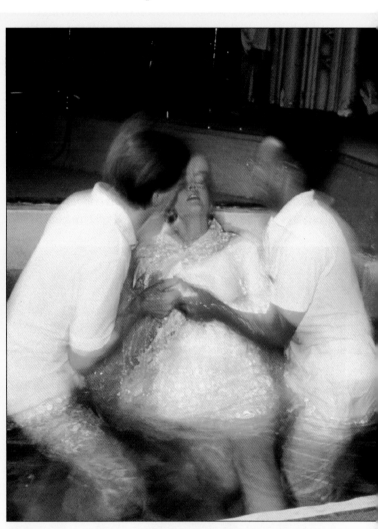

2 Look at the photograph carefully before you answer these questions.

a To which Church is this person most likely to belong?
b Why do you think the woman is wearing white clothes?
c Why is it important that the person is an adult?
d What do the people present at the baptism believe about the ceremony?

What is a Christian wedding?

Less than 1 in 10 people in the UK go to church regularly and yet 50 per cent of the population choose to marry in a church. Can you guess why? People who marry in church go through a Christian ceremony which makes several important statements about Christian marriage.

The marriage service

There are many traditions attached to marriage which have little or no religious significance – the father giving the bride away, the choice of best man etc. These traditions are just additional extras; they do not have to take place. For a church wedding, there is one element which the law demands. Do you know what this is? Look at Exercise 2.

During the service, the groom places a ring on the left hand of the bride. Often she gives him a ring as well. These familiar words are then spoken:

'I give you this ring as a sign of our marriage. With my body I will honour you, all that I am I give to you, and all that I have I share with you, within the love of God, Father, Son and Holy Spirit.'

Why do they choose a ring? The ring is intended to be a token of the love between the man and woman. It is a perfect circle with no recognisable beginning or end. What does that tell you about the love that should exist between a man and a woman for the rest of their lives?

Wedding services in the Orthodox Church are rather different. The bride and the groom exchanged rings when they became engaged. During the wedding service two silver crowns, or garlands, are held above the heads of the couple before being placed on their heads. As this is happening the priest joins the hands of the two of them together and declares that they are now husband and wife. What do you think is the symbolism behind the crowns?

In many Anglican, Catholic and Orthodox services the couple then celebrate the Eucharist together. On this occasion, the rest of the congregation do not join in. It is something very special for the two people involved.

Ever since the time of Jesus, getting married and celebrating have always gone hand in hand. Remember where Jesus performed his first miracle? See John 2.1–11 if you do not know the answer. This tradition is alive and well today as family and friends come together for the reception which provides everyone with the opportunity of joining in the celebration and giving the couple a good start to their married life together.

- What are the vows in the wedding service?
- Why is the ring an important wedding symbol?
- What is distinctive about a wedding held in an Orthodox church?

This particular wedding is taking place in Africa. What do you think is essential about any wedding, no matter where it is taking place?

1 The photograph below shows a familiar wedding scene. Try to answer these questions in your own words:

a Catholics speak of marriage as a 'sacrament' although this word is not used by Anglicans or the Free Churches. Can you explain what Catholics mean when they refer to marriage in this way?
b What do you think the giving and receiving of rings mean to the couple involved?
c Little training for marriage is given. Do you think that the Church should insist that people have some sort of training before getting married?

2 These are the only words which have to be included in a church wedding service:

I, John, take you, Anne
(I, Anne, take you, John)
to be my wife (husband)
to have and to hold,
from this day forward,
for better, for worse,
for richer, for poorer,
in sickness and in health,
to love and to cherish,
till death us do part,
according to God's holy law,
and this is my solemn vow.

(Church of England Alternative
Service Book)

Write three sentences to explain what you think each of these phrases (a–d) from the vows mean:
a '...to have and to hold, from this day forward...'
b '...for better, for worse, for richer, for poorer...'
c '...to love and to cherish...'
d '...till death us do part, according to God's holy law...'
e In the past, the bride said exactly the same vows as the groom except that she also promised to obey him. Why do you think that this word is missing from the modern marriage service?

What is a Christian burial?

Have you ever been to a Christian funeral? If so, you may have found it quite unnerving and disturbing. The funeral service is the last opportunity that people have to say goodbye to someone that they have loved. Some of the most beautiful words used anywhere in Christian prayer and worship are to be found in the service which marks the end of a person's life.

What is a Christian funeral?

As death approaches, a Roman Catholic takes his or her last Holy Communion and so receives spiritual food for the 'journey'. What journey do you think that is? They are told:

'In the name of God, the almighty Father who created you.
In the name of Jesus Christ, Son of the Living God, who suffered for you.
In the name of the Holy Spirit who was poured out for you,
Go forth, faithful Christian…
May your love be with God in Zion [heaven].'

After death, the body is sprinkled with holy water by a priest dressed in white robes. White, not black – isn't that a little strange?

The funeral service opens with words taken from John 11.25–6:

'I am the resurrection and the life; he who believes in me, though he die, yet shall he live and whoever lives and believes in me shall never die.'

What promise do these words give which might be of great comfort to someone who has just lost a loved one?

During the service, both Roman Catholics and Orthodox Christians offer prayers for the dead, although these are much less common in Anglican churches and never used in Free Church services. The Orthodox Church does not recognise any difference between the living and the dead – all are members of the invisible and visible Church, which is one Church. There are several distinctive features of the Orthodox service:

- The body is washed, dressed in new clothes and placed in a coffin. The coffin lid is left open during the service so that everyone can say their own farewell to the dead person.

- Pictures of John the Baptist, Jesus and Mary are painted on a strip of cloth which is laid across the corpse's head. An icon is placed in the dead person's hands. The body is covered with a cloth to show that it is under the protection of Jesus.

In the Orthodox Liturgy there is a beautiful hymn for the dead which contains these words:

'Give rest, O Christ, to all thy servants with thy saints
Where sorrow and pain are no more, neither sighing, but life everlasting.
Thou only art immortal, the creator and maker of man,
And we are mortal, born of the earth, and unto earth shall we return, all we go down to dust.'

This prayer draws out the great difference between God and man. What is it?

- What do many Roman Catholics take before they die?
- Which Christian Churches offer prayers for the dead?
- What is distinctive about the Orthodox burial service?

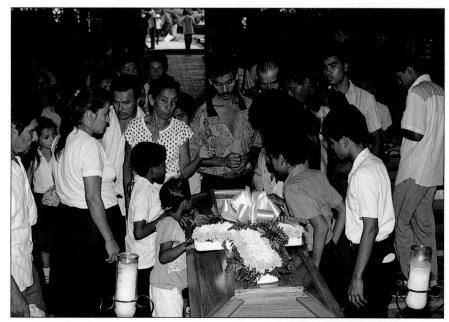

What kind of comfort do you think a priest can offer these people?

REMEMBERING WITH AFFECTION
HELENA GLADYS HAMILTON HENSMAN
ENTERED HER SAVIOUR'S PRESENCE
19TH JANUARY 1993, AGED 92.

"THEM WHICH SLEEP IN JESUS
WILL GOD BRING WITH HIM."
I. THESS. 4. 14.

1 a What sentiments about death and life after death are expressed by these two gravestones?

b Imagine that you could write your own epitaph (the inscription on the gravestone). What would you write which would sum up what you believe about death and life after death?

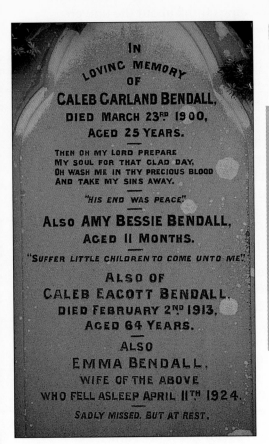

IN
LOVING MEMORY
OF
CALEB CARLAND BENDALL,
DIED MARCH 23RD 1900,
AGED 25 YEARS.

THEN OH MY LORD PREPARE
MY SOUL FOR THAT GLAD DAY,
OH WASH ME IN THY PRECIOUS BLOOD
AND TAKE MY SINS AWAY.

"HIS END WAS PEACE"

ALSO AMY BESSIE BENDALL,
AGED 11 MONTHS.

"SUFFER LITTLE CHILDREN TO COME UNTO ME"

ALSO OF
CALEB EACOTT BENDALL.
DIED FEBRUARY 2ND 1913,
AGED 64 YEARS.

ALSO
EMMA BENDALL,
WIFE OF THE ABOVE
WHO FELL ASLEEP APRIL 11TH 1924.

SADLY MISSED. BUT AT REST.

2 You can read what Jesus had to say about death and the end of time in John 11.23–5. Paul's comments on the same subjects can be found in 1 Corinthians 15.12–58. Enter some of your findings on a table like the one below:

	What will happen to each person?	What will happen at the end of time?
John 11.23–5	1	1
	2	2
	3	3
1 Corinthians 15.12–58	1	1
	2	2
	3	3
	4	4
	5	5

Add your own comments in not more than 50 words, like this:
When I die I believe that ...
When everything ends I believe that ...

3 Find out how funerals are conducted in one of the following Churches:

a the Methodist Church
b the Baptist Church
c the Quakers
d the Salvation Army

What do Christians believe about God?

There are always many questions when you begin to think about God. Do you think that God is masculine or feminine, neither or both? Is God a Spirit? Is God involved in the world? If so, how? Can people experience God? Do you think that you have ever experienced God? Would you describe your belief as a Christian one or not? If not, where has it come from?

The questions are easy to ask but the answers are much more difficult to find. Christians believe that God is deeply involved in the world in which we live and also in the details of our own lives.

The Trinity

Christians believe in:

- God the Father who has created everything.

- God the Son who is the **Saviour** of the world.

- God the Holy Spirit who brings new life and energy to those who believe in God.

This belief is called the **Trinity** – from 'tri-unity' or 'three-in-one' – and is one of the most important Christian beliefs. How can three beings be one? That's the real problem and it has been for nearly two thousand years! It is not made any easier when we discover that Christians call God the Father,

The favourite description by Jesus of God was that of a father. Why do you think that he found this a particularly useful description of God?

God the Son and God the Holy Spirit 'Persons'. How can three separate Persons not be three separate Gods? One way out of the dilemma has been to think of three spirits which are all part of the one God, united perfectly with each other in love.

We begin by looking at the Christian belief in the first member of the Trinity: God the Father.

God the Father

Christians do not believe that God is an old man with a long white beard, who spends his time somewhere between the Plough and the Milky Way! In fact, God is not a human being at all, not even one with superhuman powers. Instead God is:

- beyond all human understanding – a mystery. When human beings think about the universe many unanswerable questions come to mind. Where did the universe come from? How did life begin? What is our place in the scheme of things? Most of us feel that behind everything is mystery and Christians believe that this mystery is God.

- a force, a spirit which is everywhere at the same time but never just in one place. Jesus said that God is a Spirit, as if that answered all questions. It doesn't, of course. All that we can say is that to call God a Spirit means that God is much more like the qualities of love, peace, freedom etc. than like another human being.

- creating all things. There are two stories in the Bible about how everything began: Genesis 1 and 2. If you cannot remember what they say and how they differ, refresh your memory. Remember one thing – you are not reading about how life really started. You are reading a piece of poetry to explain that God was there working in the beginning and that God continues to work as the universe is always changing.

- best understood as our heavenly Father. Do you remember how the Lord's Prayer begins: *'Our Father, who art in heaven…'* (Matthew 6.9)

What do you think Jesus meant when he called God his 'Father'? Many people have misunderstood his words. He did not mean to imply that God is male! He had something else in mind. What do you think that was?

- What do Christians mean when they speak of God as a Trinity?
- What does it mean to speak of God as a Spirit?
- What title did Jesus teach his disciples to use of God and what did he mean by it?

The sea is often used as a picture of God. What aspect of God's character might this illuminate?

1 The Apostles and Nicene Creeds are two important early statements of Christian belief. Here is what they have to say about God:

The Apostles Creed
I believe in God, the Father almighty, Creator of heaven and earth

The Nicene Creed
We believe in one God, the Father, the almighty, maker of heaven and earth, of all that is seen and unseen.

Each of these creeds makes several statements about God. Record them, in your own words, on a table like the one below:

The Apostles Creed	The Nicene Creed
1	1
2	2
3	3

On which statements do both creeds agree?

2 Christians have always found the idea of the Trinity difficult to understand. They have often turned to pictures or illustrations to help them. Here are two such pictures:

a Do you think that either or both of these pictures are helpful in explaining the Christian belief in the Trinity? Explain why?
b Can you think of an illustration of your own for the Trinity?

What do Christians believe about Jesus Christ?

Do you think that all this talk about the Trinity makes God sound rather remote? Is belief in God something that passes you by? If so, you are in good company. Even those who are Christians are usually happier turning to Jesus as the 'human face of God'. What do you think this means?

This is Salvador Dali's famous painting of the Crucifixion. What point is he trying to make?

Jesus of Nazareth

What do Christians believe about Jesus Christ, the Son of Joseph and Mary, from Nazareth? They believe that:

- Jesus is God. Christians believe that Jesus Christ is part of the Trinity – the part that left heaven and was born as a baby in a stable in Bethlehem. The claim that God was born as a human being (an event known as the 'Incarnation') creates a series of problems. Whilst he was on earth, was Jesus God or man? The Christian answer that he was both only makes the situation more difficult to understand. Was he born like every other human being? Matthew's and Luke's Gospels say that Jesus did not have a normal human father. God was his father and he was conceived in Mary's womb by the Holy Spirit. Mary was a virgin when Jesus was conceived and born (the **Virgin Birth**).

- Jesus lived a normal life on earth. Before he emerged on to the public scene as a teacher and miracle-worker he lived like any other Jew. Then his teaching became particularly important. In it he called for total self-sacrifice. Look, for example, at these three statements:

  'Do not judge and you will not be judged.' (Matthew 7.1)
  'Love your enemies and pray for your persecutors.' (Matthew 5.44)
  'You cannot serve God and money.' (Matthew 6.24)

- Jesus was put to death by his enemies. As the Apostles Creed says:

  'He suffered under Pontius Pilate, was crucified, died and was buried.'

  As he lived a perfect life he was not dying because he had done anything wrong. He died for the sins of everyone else so that they could be forgiven by God. This is why a favourite Christian term for Jesus is 'Saviour'.

- Jesus rose from the dead. The Gospels make it clear that Jesus came back from the dead to show that he had defeated all the powers of evil.

- Jesus left the earth and returned to his Father in heaven with the promise that he would return at some future time. Christians are still waiting for this.

- What is the Virgin Birth?
- Why do Christians call Jesus their Saviour?
- What do Christians believe will happen at the end of time?

Icons of various holy subjects are popular pictures in the Orthodox Church. What do you think this icon of Jesus is intended to convey?

1 This extract is taken from the Apostles Creed. Make a list of ten things that it says about Jesus:

I believe in Jesus Christ, his only Son and Lord.
He was conceived by the power of the Holy Spirit
and born of the Virgin Mary.
He suffered under Pontius Pilate,
was crucified, died and was buried.
He descended to the dead.
On the third day he rose again.
He ascended into heaven,
and is seated on the right hand of the Father.
He will come again to judge the living and the dead.

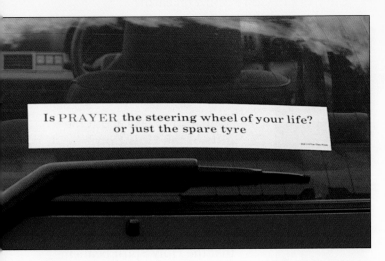

Is PRAYER the steering wheel of your life? or just the spare tyre

2 You will often see stickers like these in the back window of cars.

a What message do you think they are giving?
b Do you think that this is a good way for someone to advertise their Christian faith?
c Make up two more slogans about Jesus that might be used in car windows.

3 Here are some brief comments about Jesus gathered from a class of 13-year-olds. One speech bubble is empty so that you can add your own comment.

> Jesus was a very good teacher – one of the best that the world has seen.

> Jesus was God's Son – he brought God's message to all kinds of people.

> Jesus was a very good man. It was unfortunate that his message should have upset so many people.

> Jesus was perfect and so must have been God's Son.

> I really believe that Jesus saves us from our sins – but don't ask me how!

What do Christians believe about the Holy Spirit?

The name that Christians give to the third person in the Trinity is the Holy Spirit. For many people this conjures up eerie pictures of ghosts and things that go bump in the night. That is certainly not what Christians have in mind when they refer to the Holy Spirit.

God, the Holy Spirit

Go back again to the first chapter in the Bible. Do you remember who it was who turned a vast tract of darkness and wasteland into a beautiful world (Genesis 1.2)? It was God's Holy Spirit. The Spirit was there in the beginning, involved in God's work of creation. He crops up again and again throughout the pages of the Old Testament, doing things for God.

It should hardly surprise us to find the same thing in the New Testament. The Holy Spirit is God's agent on earth. He is at work both in the lives of individual believers and in the Christian community.

Think carefully about the following:

- When the angel Gabriel announces to Mary that she is going to have a special son she wonders how this can happen as she is not married. She is told:
'The Holy Spirit will come upon you and the power of the Most High will overshadow you.' (Luke 1.35)

The Holy Spirit is not only God's special messenger but also the means through which God's purposes are carried out.

- John the Baptist announced that when Jesus, God's **Messiah**, came he would baptise the people with the Holy Spirit rather than with water as he had done (Mark 1.8). When Jesus came to John to be baptised we are told that the Holy Spirit descended on him like a dove and remained with him throughout his life. Why a dove? Do you remember which bird it was that brought the good news to Noah that the flood waters had almost gone down (Genesis 8.12)?

- Before he was crucified, Jesus spoke to his disciples about the **Paraclete**, the Spirit, who would take his place on earth. This Greek word is usually translated as the 'helper' or 'comforter'. It can, however, mean 'counsel for the defence'. How do you think that this might tie up with the work of God's Spirit on earth?

- On the Day of Pentecost, God gave his Spirit to help the disciples preach the Good News: the Gospel. Read about this for yourself in Acts 2.

- Paul also speaks about the gifts of the Holy Spirit (1 Corinthians 12.4–11) and the fruits of the Holy Spirit (Galatians 5.12–16).

These refer to God's gifts to the Church and the fruits that the Holy Spirit bears in the lives of individual Christians. Look them up and make a list of them. You should then be in a position to understand the work that Christians believe the Holy Spirit carries out.

Christians believe that God's Holy Spirit is always with them, even when suffering for their belief. How is this shown in this picture?

- How was the Holy Spirit involved in God's work of creating the world?
- What work is the Holy Spirit given to carry out in the New Testament?
- What are the gifts and fruits of the Holy Spirit?

1 The picture above shows a stained-glass window in a modern Roman Catholic cathedral. You may have to look at it for some time before you can see what the artist is trying to say about the Holy Spirit.

a What do you think this window is trying to tell us about the Holy Spirit?
b Design your own picture based on something that you have learned about the Holy Spirit from this chapter.

2 The Nicene Creed has this to say about the Holy Spirit:

'We believe in the Holy Spirit,
the Lord, the giver of life,
who proceeds from the Father and from the Son.
With the Father and the Son he is
worshipped and glorified.
He has spoken through the Prophets.'

a Christians believe that the Holy Spirit is God in the same way as the Father and the Son. Which phrases in the Nicene Creed suggest this conclusion?
b Which phrases suggest that the Holy Spirit is God in action in the world?

What do Christians believe about suffering?

The question in the title above brings us up against the greatest mystery of all. Why do people suffer? Why do some people suffer much more than others? Why is so much suffering undeserved? Why are so many babies born mentally or physically handicapped? Why do some people die quickly whilst others suffer long, drawn-out and very painful deaths?

Dealing with suffering

Questions like these will worry all of us at some time or other. They will probably hit us most sharply when someone we love suffers acutely or when we come up against personal suffering for the first time. Suffering is a fact of life for most people at some time. No human being escapes it altogether. For many people it destroys all possibility of believing in a loving God. They say 'Why, if there is a loving God, does he allow such suffering?' Others turn to God to see them through their suffering and pain. They say 'I don't know what I'd do if I didn't have God to see me through.' Everyone's reaction is an intensely personal one.

You might like to think for a moment or two about these two attitudes. How do you think you might react when suffering hits you for the first time?

Newspapers are full of examples of suffering. Collect as many examples as you can. Do you think that suffering can simply be divided into deserved suffering or undeserved suffering? If so, does this distinction help those who believe in God?

The problem of evil

You can find examples of evil and suffering all around you. Consider each of the headlines on the page opposite in the light of these questions:

Why does God allow suffering?

Why doesn't God do something about suffering?

If God is able and willing to do something about suffering, why does it exist?

To what extent have human beings contributed towards the sum total of suffering?

Christians have been trying to respond to questions like these for centuries. Amongst the many answers that they have come up with have been the following:

- That much suffering is caused by human selfishness (sin). Sin is a part of human nature – you don't have to teach a young child to do wrong. Take, for example, the motorist who, driving carelessly kills two children, or the man who smokes 40 cigarettes a day for 30 years and dies of lung cancer. You don't have to think hard to find someone to blame in these instances, do you?

- Suffering is part of life. You cannot have one without the other. When people suffer they grow as human beings and find inner resources to cope with that suffering. Just try to imagine, for a moment, a world without suffering. We would have little left to fight or struggle for. Is that true?

- As long as people have free will, there will always be suffering. Everyday we make many decisions which force us to choose between good and evil. Inevitably we sometimes take the wrong course and then we suffer the consequences. Can you think of any examples of this?

- God suffers alongside those who suffer. After

For most people life seems to be a mystery from the word 'go'. Do you agree?

Town whose senses are dead to slaughter

Consultant shot in back by boy he tried to help

Tutsi refugees call for world help to halt massacres

Seven killed as poison cloud engulfs flats

32 die as rain sweeps Europe

Elderly and children could not escape from the river of fire

Italy declares flood mourning day

Reagan reveals he is suffering from Alzheimer's

Mother said no to cancer treatment to save unborn son

Briton sees his wife swept to death in flood

all, Jesus, God's Son, was tortured and put to death. Yet light followed darkness as Jesus rose from the dead. Sickness and suffering are mysteries which must be accepted now. One day everything will be explained.

Do these explanations answer most of the questions about suffering or not? The probability is that you will be thinking about them for the rest of your life.

- Does human selfishness and sin explain all suffering?
- What is the link between free will and suffering?
- When do Christians believe that God suffered?

1 Someone has said that only those people who have experienced suffering at first hand can really talk about it. Do you think that this is true? These comments are made by people who know about suffering from the inside:

Lee, a paraplegic, aged 29
'I know what it is like to lose my health through no fault of my own. For a long time I felt very bitter and angry. Then I realised that I could not stay that way for the rest of my life. The only thing to do with a disability is to fight it with all your strength – without lapsing into self-pity.'

Jenny, a blind person, aged 25
'I was born blind. That helped me in a way. I can't look back wistfully to a time when I could see. Strangely enough, being blind does have some compensations – I'll leave you to work out what they might be!'

Mike, a muscular dystrophy sufferer, aged 35
'I suffer from a disease for which there is no known cure. I am going to get worse, I know that. Yet I believe in God and do not know how I would cope with my illness without that faith. It makes all the difference to me.'

There is a lot for you to think about here. Try to imagine yourself in the situation of each person speaking. How do you think you would cope? Would a faith in God help you to cope or not?

2 Here are two questions to really make you think:

a If God is both all-loving and all-powerful, why doesn't he intervene to prevent suffering?
b Could suffering be sent by God as a punishment or to prepare people for heaven?

Index

Page references in bold indicate that the word is defined on this page in the 'For your dictionary' box.